T0311715

Cambridge Elements ≡

Elements in the Philosophy of Mind
edited by
Keith Frankish
The University of Sheffield

IMAGINATION AND CREATIVE THINKING

Amy Kind
Claremont McKenna College

CAMBRIDGE
UNIVERSITY PRESS

University Printing House, Cambridge CB2 8BS, United Kingdom

One Liberty Plaza, 20th Floor, New York, NY 10006, USA

477 Williamstown Road, Port Melbourne, VIC 3207, Australia

314–321, 3rd Floor, Plot 3, Splendor Forum, Jasola District Centre, New Delhi – 110025, India

103 Penang Road, #05–06/07, Visioncrest Commercial, Singapore 238467

Cambridge University Press is part of the University of Cambridge.

It furthers the University's mission by disseminating knowledge in the pursuit of education, learning, and research at the highest international levels of excellence.

www.cambridge.org
Information on this title: www.cambridge.org/9781108977227
DOI: 10.1017/9781108973335

© Amy Kind 2022

This publication is in copyright. Subject to statutory exception and to the provisions of relevant collective licensing agreements, no reproduction of any part may take place without the written permission of Cambridge University Press.

First published 2022

A catalogue record for this publication is available from the British Library.

ISBN 978-1-108-97722-7 Paperback
ISSN 2633-9080 (online)
ISSN 2633-9072 (print)

Additional resources for this publication at www.cambridge.org/kind_resources

Cambridge University Press has no responsibility for the persistence or accuracy of URLs for external or third-party internet websites referred to in this publication and does not guarantee that any content on such websites is, or will remain, accurate or appropriate.

Imagination and Creative Thinking

Elements in the Philosophy of Mind

DOI: 10.1017/9781108973335
First published online: July 2022

Amy Kind
Claremont McKenna College
Author for correspondence: Amy Kind, akind@cmc.edu

Abstract: This Element explores the nature of both imagination and creative thinking in an effort to understand the relation between them and also to understand their role in the vast array of activities in which they are typically implicated, from art, music, and literature to technology, medicine, and science. Focusing on the contemporary philosophical literature, it takes up several interrelated questions: What is imagination, and how does it fit into the cognitive architecture of the mind? What is creativity? Is imagination required for creativity? Is creativity required for imagination? Is a person simply born either imaginative or not (and likewise, either creative or not), or are imagination and creativity skills that can be cultivated? And finally, are imagination and creativity uniquely human capacities, or can they be had by nonbiological entities such as AI systems?

This Element also has a video abstract: www.cambridge.org/kind_abstract

Keywords: imagination, creativity, discovery, genius, creative machines

© Amy Kind 2022

ISBNs: 9781108977227 (PB), 9781108973335 (OC)
ISSNs: 2633-9080 (online), 2633-9072 (print)

Contents

1 Introduction

Both imagination and creative thinking are typically implicated in a vast array of activities – from the domains of art, music, and literature to those of technology, medicine, and science. Moreover, both imagination and creative thinking are typically seen as essential to the success of these activities. When we're talking about renowned artists like Michelangelo or renowned scientists like Albert Einstein, we often point to their capacities for imagination and creative thinking as the key drivers behind their tremendous achievements. Or consider Leonardo da Vinci, a true Renaissance man whose many celebrated contributions range from art to anatomy, from architecture to astronomy. Heralded as one of the world's greatest geniuses, da Vinci is generally said to have had prodigious powers of imagination that were well ahead of his time. As philosopher Alan White has written, "Great thinkers are often imaginative thinkers because they can free themselves from the rut of the actual and ride on the uncharted trails of the possible" (White 1990, 186).

This Element explores the mental activities of imagination and creative thinking in an effort to gain a better understanding of what they are and how they work. That said, this is not a how-to guide. If you're looking for *Ten Life Hacks that Will Make You More Imaginative!* or *How to Become a Creative Genius Overnight!* You'll unfortunately have to look elsewhere. Leaving the world of clickbait behind, we'll instead dive into the philosophical literature in an attempt to address several interrelated questions: What is imagination, and how does it fit into the cognitive architecture of the mind? What is creativity? Is imagination required for creativity? Is creativity required for imagination? Is a person simply born either imaginative or not (and likewise, either creative or not), or can imagination and creativity be cultivated? And finally, are imagination and creativity uniquely human capacities, or can they be had by nonbiological entities such as artificial intelligence (AI) systems?

2 What Is Imagination?

Imagination can be thought of as a speculative mental activity. It allows us to speculate about how matters might in some way be different from how they in fact are. As Shen-yi Liao and Tamar Gendler define it in their entry on imagination in the *Stanford Encyclopedia of Philosophy*: "To imagine is to represent without aiming at things as they actually, presently, and subjectively are" (Liao and Gendler 2019). We see similar definitions in the psychological literature. To give just one example, Marjorie Taylor characterizes imagination as "the capacity to mentally transcend time, place, and/or circumstance" (Taylor 2013, 3).

To help us better understand the nature of this speculative mental activity, it will be useful to have some examples before us. Let's start with three vignettes:

> *Pretend Pirates.* Penny and Priya are climbing one of the play structures in the park when they decide to pretend to be pirates. All of the play structures become pirate ships, and the kids climbing on the other structures become members of rival pirate gangs. The grass becomes the ocean, and the sandbox becomes an island where they think the treasure has been buried. They talk to one another excitedly: How much treasure do you think there is? How can we get there before the other pirates?

> *Decorating Decisions.* Dave's in the process of making redecorating plans for his living room. Having collected paint chips and furniture catalogs and measured the space, he now reflects on the important decisions he has to make and turns the issues over in his mind. Which shade of cream-colored paint would be a better choice for the walls, natural calico or almost oyster? Should I purchase a loveseat or a chaise lounge? Would it look better if the tall bookcase were positioned against the south wall, or should it stay against the north wall?

> *Empathetic Explorations.* Emily is making her lunch in the kitchen at work when she witnesses a tense exchange between her coworkers Ellen and Eddie. Looking at them, she tries to understand what they're each feeling. Does that expression on Eddie's face mean he's angry or upset? How would I feel if Ellen had made those critical comments to me?

In each of these vignettes, imagination seems to play a crucial role in the activities being undertaken. When Penny and Priya are taking the sandbox to be an island, it's likely that they do so by imagining it as such. In thinking about the buried treasure, they are likely imagining a treasure chest, bursting at its seams with golden coins. Likewise, a natural way for Dave to decide which paint to choose would be on the basis of imaginatively comparing the living room walls covered with the two different colors. And finally, the way that Emily figures out what Ellen and Eddie are feeling is most likely by way of imaginative projection. She puts herself in each of their shoes, so to speak.

Pretending, decision-making, and empathizing are just some of the many everyday activities in which we rely on imagination. We also use imagination to engage with fiction, to problem solve, and to try to figure out where we left our car keys! An athlete might call upon imagination to better prepare for their next competition, while a chef might use imagination to decide which spices to add to the dish they're preparing. In fact, once we start to think about it, we're naturally led to a sense that imagination is ubiquitous. It's hard to see how even a day could go by without its use.

But these ubiquitous uses of imagination differ from one another in various ways. Sometimes we imagine that a certain scenario is true, as when Penny and Priya imagine that the play structures are pirate ships. But sometimes we simply imagine objects, as when Penny and Priya imagine the buried treasure. This suggests that there are structural differences among imaginings, that is, differences relating to the way the content is structured. Imaginings also differ in terms of their modality. In the first two of our vignettes, for example, the imaginative acts employed seem naturally understood as acts of visual imagination. In using the playground structures as props in their imaginings, Penny and Priya visually imagine them to look different from how they in fact do, and they also form mental images of the treasure they take to be buried beneath the sand. Likewise, Dave forms mental images of the walls painted with the alternative paint colors. In the third vignette, however, the imaginative acts don't seem to be visual in nature. Instead, they're most naturally understood as acts of emotional or experiential imagination. Emily imaginatively recreates the kinds of emotions and experiences that her coworkers might be undergoing.

As these brief remarks suggest, imagining comes in importantly different varieties. But let's also note an additional way that we can distinguish imaginings from one another. In the first vignette, Penny and Priya are engaged in a fanciful activity with no real practical purpose. They're aiming to escape from the reality in which they find themselves. But the activities in the second and third vignettes are not fanciful. They do have practical purposes. Both Dave and Emily are aiming to understand something about the reality in which they find themselves. So not only does imagining come in different varieties but it can also be employed with importantly different aims. In what follows, we'll explore each of these differences in turn.

2.1 Varieties of Imagining

Philosophers working on imagination have adopted numerous different taxonomies in an effort to understand its nature.[1] In fact, when trying to make sense of the different taxonomies on offer, one might be tempted to conclude that there are as many taxonomies as there are philosophers working on imagination! Nonetheless, the following division of imagination into two broad types should be relatively uncontroversial.

---

[1] To give just a couple of examples, see Neil Van Leeuwen's distinction between constructive, attitudinal, and imagistic imagination (2013) or Gregory Currie and Ian Ravenscroft's distinction between creative and recreative imagination (2002).

2.1.1 Propositional Imagining

First we have what's typically called *propositional imagination*. As part of the scenario depicted in our Pretend Pirates vignette, Penny and Priya might each imagine that the rival pirate gang is going to beat them to the buried treasure. Worried about how he is going to pay for his living room renovation, Dave might imagine that he wins the lottery as part of the scenario depicted in Decorating Decisions. In each of these imaginings, the content of the imagining is a proposition. Propositional imagining is thus classified as a propositional attitude akin to other propositional attitudes such as belief, desire, and intention. As a general matter, one can take many different attitudes toward the same propositional content. So just as Dave might imagine that he wins the lottery, he might also believe that he wins the lottery, desire that he wins the lottery, hope that he wins the lottery, and so on.

Philosophers have had lots to say about what distinguishes propositional imagining from other propositional attitudes (see, e.g., Gendler 2003; Nichols 2004). In doing so, they have concentrated most of their attention on differences between propositional imagination and belief. Though these differences may seem obvious – in line with William James' remark that "Everyone knows the difference between imagining a thing and believing in its existence" (James 1889) – it will nonetheless be helpful to make these points explicit.

Some of the differences can be cashed out in functional terms, as imagining and believing tend to play different functional roles in our overall mental life. For example, when someone imagines that there are dangerous pirates on the playground, they are unlikely to call for help or seek out the police. Matters would be different were they to *believe* that there are dangerous pirates on the playground. So imagining and believing have different functional roles with respect to action guidance. They also seem to play different roles with respect to our affective systems, that is, with respect to emotion. Imagining that there are dangerous pirates on the playground is unlikely to cause someone to be terrified. Again, matters would be different were this proposition to be believed rather than imagined.

One might also distinguish imagination and belief in terms of their voluntariness. Consider the exchange that ensues in Lewis Carroll's *Through the Looking Glass* after the Queen tells Alice that she's over 100 years old (to be precise, that she's "one hundred and one, five months and a day"):

> "I can't believe that!" said Alice.
> "Can't you?" the Queen said in a pitying tone. "Try again: draw a long breath, and shut your eyes."

> Alice laughed. "There's no use trying," she said: "one can't believe impossible things."
>
> "I daresay you haven't had much practice," said the Queen. "When I was your age, I always did it for half-an-hour a day. Why, sometimes I've believed as many as six impossible things before breakfast."[2]

Philosophers tend to side with Alice here: One can't make oneself believe something by sheer force of will. If you don't believe that you are at a tea party with a talking rabbit, you can't make yourself come to hold that belief simply by closing your eyes and trying harder, no matter how long you try or how much you practice (see, e.g., Williams 1973). But now compare imagining. It's remarkably easy to imagine that you are at a tea party with a talking rabbit. In fact, I bet that many readers did so just in virtue of having read the previous sentence. (If you didn't, re-read the last sentence and try again.) Imagining, unlike belief, is a voluntary activity. It is subject to the will.[3]

This point about voluntariness relates to a further distinction between imagination and belief concerning their relationship to truth. Belief is often said to have a special connection to truth, namely, that it aims at the truth. That's not to say that we can't have false beliefs. Alas, many of us have far too many of those. But as a general matter, when it comes to belief formation we try (or should try) to acquire only true ones. Likewise for belief maintenance. When we discover we have a false belief, we discard it. Matters are quite different with respect to imagining. Even when there are no pirates on the playground, there's nothing wrong with Penny and Priya each imagining that there are. Granted, we may and often do imagine true things. When trying to find my lost keys, I might imagine that they are hidden under some papers on my desk – and, lo and behold, sometimes that imagining gets it right! But we may and often do imagine false things as well, even things we know full well to be false. Unlike belief, imagining does not seem to have any special connection to truth one way or the other.[4]

Despite these differences between propositional imagination and belief, there's at least one important respect in which the propositional imaginings we've thus far considered seem to be more like belief than like other propositional desires such as desire and hope. This can be best understood by way of the philosophical notion of *direction of fit*. Attitudes like belief have what's called *mind-to-world* direction of fit, whereas attitudes like desire have what's

---

[2] The full text of *Through the Looking Glass* is freely available through Project Gutenberg at www.gutenberg.org/files/12/12-h/12-h.htm

[3] Dorsch (2012) develops an agency-based theory of imagination on which its voluntariness plays a crucial role.

[4] For further discussion, see Sinhababu 2016.

called *world-to-mind* direction of fit. For beliefs, we try to fit our mind to the world; for desires, we try to fit the world to our mind. When forming a belief, our aim is met when the representational content matches with the world. (As should be obvious, this point connects very closely to the point just made about the special connection between belief and truth.) In contrast, when forming a desire, our aim is met when the world matches with the representational content. Propositional attitudes with world-to-mind direction of fit, including desires but also hopes and intentions, cannot be appropriately described in terms of truth and falsity. These notions don't apply to them. Rather, these propositional attitudes are more appropriately described as either satisfied or unsatisfied. When the world fits one's mind, the desire (or hope or intention) is satisfied; when the world does not fit one's mind, the desire (or hope or intention) is unsatisfied.

As we've seen, propositional imaginings differ from beliefs in that they need not aim to represent the actual world around us. But they nonetheless seem to be more like belief than like desire when it comes to direction of fit. We can see propositional imagining as having something like a mind-to-world direction of fit, perhaps, if we take the relevant world to be a particular imaginary world (or a particular possible world). Alternatively, we might be better able to capture the relevant similarity between propositional imagination and belief, and their difference from attitudes like desire, in terms of a distinction drawn by Nishi Shah and David Velleman (2005). On Shah and Velleman's view, we can best understand attitudes like belief and desire in terms of a distinction between attitudes that treat their contents as *true* and attitudes that treat their contents as something that is *to be made true*. Imagining and belief both fall into the first class, whereas desire falls into the second. Though an imagining need not aim at the truth, it nonetheless treats its content as true – or at least, true for the purposes of the relevant imaginative exercise.

Recently, some philosophers have argued that we should also recognize a different kind of propositional imagining that is more like desire than like belief. This kind of imagining is sometimes referred to as *desire-like imagining* (Currie 2002) and sometimes as *imaginative desire*, or *i-desire* for short (Doggett and Egan 2007). The basic idea is something like this: Just as we sometimes explore beliefs that we don't really hold by imagining their content in a belief-like way, we also sometimes explore desires that we don't really have by imagining their content in a desire-like way. For example, when Penny and Priya are pretending to be pirates, just as they might have a belief-like imagining that the other kids are pirates, they might have a desire-like imagining to kill all the other pirates in a sword fight. It's this desire-like imagining that causes them to yell things like, "Die, evil pirates, die!" and to thrust the tree branches they're holding (i.e., their swords) at the other kids. Supposing that Penny and Priya are good, non-homicidal children, it seems unlikely that they really want to kill all the other kids in a sword fight. Rather, according to proponents of i-desires, this is just something that they *imaginatively want*. Importantly, imaginatively wanting something isn't meant to be imagining (in a belief-like way) that you want something; it's being in an imaginative state of wanting.

The existence of i-desires is highly controversial. I myself am skeptical about their existence, as I think there are all sorts of ordinary desires that we can invoke to explain what's going on with Penny and Priya without having to postulate i-desires (Kind 2011; see also Spaulding 2015). For example, Penny and Priya want (actually want, not imaginatively want) to act like pirates. They also want (actually want, not imaginatively want) the pretense to incorporate the murder of the other pirates. To my mind, we can explain everything we need to explain about Penny and Priya's actions – why they yell what they do, why they move as they do – without needing any recourse to i-desires, and the postulation of this novel kind of propositional imagining thus strikes me as unmotivated. But I won't explore this debate any further here. Our main goal in this Element is to explore the connections between imagination and creativity. For this purpose, desire-like imagination would not be particularly relevant even were it to exist.

2.1.2 Sensory Imagination

The second type of imagination we will consider is sensory imagination. To understand sensory imagination, it will be helpful to focus first on what's often referred to as *imagistic imagination*. Let's return to our Decorating Decisions vignette. When Dave asks himself which shade of cream-colored paint would work best on the walls, the imaginative act in which he engages to answer the question will likely proceed by way of visual mental imagery. He visually imagines the walls painted in natural calico, then visually imagines them painted in almost oyster, and mentally compares the two in an effort to come to a decision.

In referring to this kind of imagining as imagistic imagination, we need to be careful. Though the notion of "image" often has a visual connotation, in the sense here intended it is meant to apply across sensory modalities. Dave's imagining is a visual one, but there are parallel imaginings corresponding to all the other senses as well. A musician working on composing a sonata might auditorily imagine how the notes in a given measure sound. A novice perfumer might be presented with various formulas as part of their on-the-job training and tasked with olfactorily imagining how they smell. A parent doing some online shopping for clothing for a child with sensory sensitivities might tactilely imagine how the shirt they are considering for purchase feels against the skin. It's thus important to be clear that we can talk of auditory, olfactory, gustatory, and tactile images along with visual images.

As this brief discussion suggests, while propositional imagination was best understood on analogy with belief, imagistic imagination is best understood on analogy with perception.[5] One way to bring out the analogy is to consider the phenomenology of both activities. Imagistically imagining a basketball has a similar phenomenal feel to seeing a basketball. There are differences of course. Hume (1739/1985) famously described the difference in terms of force and vivacity – the imagining is said to be less forceful and/or less vivid than the perceptual experience.[6] But they nonetheless share a significant degree of phenomenal similarity – so significant, in fact, that in rare cases one of these mental activities might even be mistaken for the other (Perky 1910).

Of course, the analogy to perception is not a perfect one. Like propositional imagination, imagistic imagination is subject to the will. Typically, all one has to do in order to imagistically imagine a given object or scenario is to set oneself the task of doing so. But just as this feature of will-dependence sets propositional imagination apart from belief despite other ways in which they are analogous, this feature of will-dependence sets imagistic imagination apart from perception despite other ways in which they are analogous. Though I can't make myself perceive a monkey simply by willing myself to do so, I can make myself visually imagine a monkey simply by willing myself to do so.

There's one important caveat. As first noticed by Francis Galton in the late nineteenth century, some individuals find themselves hard-pressed to produce detailed or clear mental imagery, and some even claim to be completely unable to produce voluntary mental imagery (Galton 1880). This phenomenon, now often called *aphantasia*, is still not very well understood, despite having received increased attention in recent years (see, e.g., Zeman, Dewar, and Sala 2015). But insofar as an individual has a deficit with respect to the voluntary production of mental imagery, they will have a corresponding deficit with respect to imagistic imagination and will not necessarily be able to engage in acts of imagistic imagination simply by willing themselves to do so.

The will-dependence of imagistic imagination goes hand in hand with another feature of it, namely, its lack of world sensitivity. Here again we can contrast imagination and perception. Perception is world-sensitive. When the

---

[5] For a helpful discussion comparing and contrasting imagination and perception, see Nanay 2016.
[6] See Kind 2017 for reservations about this way of putting the point.

sights and sounds of the world around you change, your perceptions will change accordingly. Perception tracks these changes. It is sensitive to them. Imagination, in contrast, is not. Suppose that I am looking at my dogs who are sleeping on the couch. When the doorbell rings, they perk up, jump off the couch, and run to the front door. I no longer perceive them sleeping on the couch – I can't, as they're not there. But I can imagine them sleeping on the couch. Though my perception of them changes as their activity changes, my imagining of them need not. In line with our opening characterization of imagination, imagistic imagination allows us to represent things or situations other than as they in fact are. This point is often put by connecting imagination with possibility or, more specifically, by drawing a useful analogy: Imagination is to the possible as perception is to the actual.

With this sketch of imagistic imagination before us, now recall our third vignette, Empathetic Explorations. When Emily overhears the argument between Ellen and Eddie, she tries to imagine how each of them is feeling. This involves imagining emotions and other affective states. At other times she might also imagine feeling cold, or feeling pain, or feeling hungry. These kinds of imaginative exercises don't seem to be directly analogous to either belief or perception. Rather, they seem to be analogous to experience. To handle these cases, it looks like we should posit a third form of imagining, *experiential imagining*, that contrasts with both propositional and imagistic imagining.

Though it is important to include experiential imagining within our conception of imagination, philosophical discussion often treats experiential imagining within the same category as imagistic imagination. In practice, then, the three-way distinction that holds between propositional, imagistic, and experiential imagination generally collapses into a two-way distinction between propositional imagination and the other two combined. One reason that it's natural to group imagistic imagination and experiential imagination together, and to contrast them with propositional imagination, is that neither of these forms of imagining takes a propositional form.

Some philosophers have attempted to further motivate this grouping by suggesting that imagistic imagining is a subtype of experiential imagining. In Decorating Decisions, for example, Dave's imagistic imagining of his living room walls might be thought of us as an imagining of the experience of seeing them. This way of viewing the relationship between imagistic imagination and experiential imagination is common among those who adopt a simulationist approach to imagination, that is, those who see all imaginative states as simulations of other mental states (for one influential defense of simulationism, see Currie and Ravenscroft 2002).

Personally, I prefer a different way of motivating the practice of grouping imagistic and experiential imagining together. Recall that we have already stretched the notion of mental image so that it extends beyond the visual case. In my view, there's no harm in stretching it a bit farther, moving beyond the sensory domain so that we can think of pain imagery, emotional imagery, and other kinds of "feeling" imagery as being involved in experiential imagining. Once we do that, we can treat experiential imagining as a subtype of imagistic imagining. I will adopt this practice in this Element, and going forward I will refer to them both under the category of *sensory imagination*.

Before closing this discussion of sensory imagination, I should note some commonalities it shares with propositional imagination. Two of the key features of sensory imagination that we have discussed – its voluntariness and its lack of world sensitivity – are also features of propositional imagination. Just as we come to engage in sensory imagining by sheer force of will, and just as that imagining need not track the features of the world around it, we can come to engage in non-world-sensitive propositional imagining by sheer force of will. I can imagine two peacefully sleeping dogs, and I can imagine that two dogs are sleeping peacefully, even if the dogs I am imagining are in fact maniacally jumping up and down and barking at the front door. These two features are also indicative of a third commonality, namely, that both propositional imagination and imagistic imagination are mental *activities*. The fact that imagining is subject to the will shows us that imagining is something that we do, not something that just happens to us.

In my view, there is an additional commonality as well. As is widely agreed among philosophers of imagination, images are often involved in some way in propositional imaginings as well as in sensory imaginings. When Penny and Priya imagine that all the play structures in the park are pirate ships, they will likely mentally superimpose pirate-paraphernalia on the play structure as they look at it – a flag with skull-and-crossbones, loaded cannons, barrels of rum, and a giant tattered sail. The way that they imagine the relevant proposition, in other words, is by producing mental images of what the proposition represents. Are these mental images merely incidental to the act of propositional imagining? Could they make do equally well without them? Many philosophers would answer in the affirmative. Such philosophers believe that imagination – in particular, propositional imagination – can occur without imagery. (See, for example, Walton 1990; Van Leeuwen 2013; Stokes 2019.) I disagree. There are many ways to speculatively consider a proposition. One might propositionally imagine it, but one also might suppose it or conceive it. What makes the speculative consideration an act of imagining rather than one of these other mental activities? To my mind, the best way to answer this question is to invoke mental imagery (Kind 2001; see also Brann 1991). What differentiates propositional imagination from sensory imagination is not that imagery is essentially involved in the one and not the other but rather that these two varieties of imagination take different forms. The difference between imagining my dogs sleeping on the couch and imagining that my dogs are sleeping on the couch is not that the first involves imagery while the second does not, but rather that the second involves imagining something that is propositional in form while the first does not.

Why do some philosophers deny that propositional imagining must involve imagery? Two different kinds of cases have been offered in the imagination literature. First, some philosophers point to cases where an image itself is not sufficient to distinguish between two different scenarios that might be imagined. To give just one example, Alan White suggests that "imagery of a sailor scrambling ashore could be exactly the same as that of his twin brother crawling backwards into the sea, yet to imagine one of these is quite different from imagining the other" (White 1990, 92). Second, some philosophers point to cases where it does not seem possible for an image to capture the imagined scenario. Again, to give just one example, Neil Van Leeuwen suggests that "When I imagine, on reading *Lord of the Rings*, that elves can live forever, I'm fictionally imagining a proposition that I couldn't imagine using mental imagery. It would take too long!" (Van Leeuwen 2013, 22).

In both instances, however, the purported counterexamples derive their apparent force from a misunderstanding of what it means to say that propositional imagining essentially involves mental imagery. In making this claim, one needn't be saying that the image involved in an imagining must be sufficient to distinguish that imagining from all other possible imaginings. The fact that one might use the very same image to imagine Susan the sailor and her twin sister Sally does not show that the images aren't essentially involved in the imagining. The only reason to think that would be if one required that every element of the imagined scenario had to be fully captured by the image content. Call this the *read-off requirement*: When imagining a scenario imagistically, every element of the imagined scenario must be able to be read off the image. It doesn't take much reflection to see that the read-off requirement is implausible. In typical cases, the image I use when imagining Susan won't be able to differentiate it from an imagining of a mere Susan-façade. But my imagining of Susan is an imagining of a person, not a façade, even though her personhood cannot be directly read off the image. As this example suggests, unless we are going to deny that images can *ever* be involved in imaginings, it looks like the read-off requirement is far too strong.[7]

---

[7] For further discussion and a more developed argument in favor of the claim that imagining essentially involves imagery, see Kind 2001. For a different kind of defense of the claim that not all of the content of an image needs to be read off the image, see Kung 2010, in particular his discussion of the distinction between intrinsic and assigned content.

Once we reject the read-off requirement, however, the proposed counter-examples lose their bite. In imagining that elves live forever, I might produce an image of twelve generations of elves gathering for a family photo. Or I might produce an image of a page in my family photo album containing pictures of the same youthful looking elf at my great-grandparents' wedding, at my grandparents' wedding, at my parents' wedding, and at my wedding. Is it built into these images that the elf lives forever, as opposed to just a very long time? No. Is it built into the image that this is a general claim about elves? No. Do either of these facts show that the imagining doesn't essentially involve the image? Also no.

To more fully defuse the force of the proposed counterexamples, I need to make a further point. For while my discussion thus far suggests ways that these imaginings *can* involve imagery, one might reasonably think that I have not yet established that all imaginings *must* involve imagery. Though I don't have the space here to make the case in full, I think that the need to adopt an imagery-based account of imagination can be motivated in large part by contrasting imagining with other speculative activities such as supposing and conceiving. If we want to see these activities as different from one another – and there seems good reason to do so, since they seem to play different roles in epistemology (Balcerak Jackson 2016)– then an imagery-based account of imagination makes good sense.[8]

In what follows, this account will often be in the background of my discussion. Thinking about imagination – all imagination, not just sensory imagination – as essentially involving mental imagery helps to cement a stronger connection with creativity.[9] But nothing I'll say presupposes the imagery-based account of imagination. In particular, when I turn in Section 4 to the relation between imagination and creativity, I will try to be neutral about whether the imagining in question involves imagery or not. Before we turn to creativity, however, we need to look more closely at two very different aims that one might have when engaging in an act of imagination. As we will see, both of these aims prove to be relevant in understanding the relationship between imagination and creativity.

2.2 Aims of Imagining

Let's return once more to our second vignette. As we described the Decorating Decisions scenario, Dave is engaging in the imaginative acts described for

---

[8] For a detailed discussion of the differences between imagining and supposing, see Weinberg and Meskin 2006, 191–197.

[9] Peter Langland-Hassan disagrees; see Langland-Hassan 2020, 264.

a very practical purpose: He's in the midst of redecorating his living room, and he needs to make some important decisions. He needs to select a paint color. He needs to purchase some additional seating for the space, be it a loveseat or a chaise lounge. He needs to rearrange the furniture. When he imagines the walls painted in almost oyster, he's doing so in an effort to decide whether he likes the way it looks, and whether he likes this imagined scenario better than the one where the walls were painted in natural calico. Likewise for when he imagines a particular loveseat or chaise lounge.

But now let's consider a slightly different scenario. Suppose Dave's friend Fred comes over and ends up leafing through the furniture catalog. Fred is living in a small apartment and doesn't have any plans to redecorate it anytime soon; he's perfectly happy with his old comfortable couch, and, in any case, he doesn't have the money to purchase any new furniture. Still, the next day, while he's in a boring meeting at work, he finds himself imagining some of the sofas from the catalog in his own living room. He finds it surprisingly entertaining to picture the elaborate and expensive pieces in his own space, and he finds it helps pass the time while his colleagues drone on.

Dave's imaginings and Fred's imaginings might be similar in form and content, yet they are very different from one another in aim. Though Dave's imaginative acts are all in the service of decision-making, Fred's are merely whimsical ways of passing the time. This difference in aims guides the content of the imaginings as they continue. For example, as Fred's imaginative activity unfolds, he might go on to imagine the Iron Throne[10] in his living room and then replace it with the captain's chair[11] from the *Enterprise*, and then the iconic egg chairs[12] from *Men in Black*. While these fanciful explorations fit perfectly well with Fred's imaginative aims, they would not be well suited to the aims that guide Dave's imagining.

This difference in aims might also be characterized by noting that Dave and Fred are putting imagination to two very different uses. To call upon terminology that I introduced in a piece co-written with Peter Kung, sometimes imagination is put to what we might call an *instructive use*, one in which the imaginer aims to learn something about the world as it is. At other times, imagination is put to what we might call a *transcendent use*, one in which the imaginer aims to transcend or escape the world as it is (Kind and Kung 2016).

The fact that imagination can be put to such different uses might initially seem to present us with something of a puzzle.[13] How can an activity that

---

[10] https://gameofthrones.fandom.com/wiki/Iron_Throne
[11] https://memory-alpha.fandom.com/wiki/Command_chair
[12] https://filmandfurniture.com/2017/12/scene-nowt-chair-taken-ovalia-egg-chair-men-black/
[13] Kung and I refer to this as *the puzzle of imaginative use* (Kind and Kung 2016).

enables us to escape from the world around us also enable us to learn anything significant about the world around us? To give this worry a bit more bite, consider a feature of imagining that we noted in our discussion in Section 2.1.1: Imagining is not world-sensitive. In fact, this feature of imagining seems to be critically important for its transcendent use. It's precisely because imagination need not track the reality around us that it enables us to escape that reality. But the fact that imagining is not world-sensitive seems to present something of an obstacle to its instructive use. How can imagining teach us anything of significance about the real world if it does not track reality and can depart from it?

To dissolve this puzzle, we need to attend to the fact that imaginers need not be passive observers of their imaginings. As we've noted, imagining is subject to the will and thus under our control. In transcendent uses of imagination, however, we exercise this control differently from how we exercise it in instructive uses. Transcendent uses of imagining are typically marked by a kind of unshackling. We shrug off the shackles of reality and see what's possible. Assuming your neighborhood is anything like mine, your local children's park doesn't contain pirate ships outfitted with loaded cannons and barrels of rum, nor is it the site of a sword fight between rival pirate gangs. But that's no bar to the park existing exactly that way in imagination. Assuming your living room is anything like mine, it doesn't contain an Iron Throne. But again, that's no bar to its being furnished that way in imagination. Instructive uses, in contrast, are not typically marked with this kind of rampant unshackling. In instructive uses, we tend to tether ourselves fairly tightly to reality.

I find it helpful to put this basic point in terms of constraints: Imagination can be constrained in all sorts of ways (see Kind 2016, 2018). Typically, we do not impose many constraints when engaging in transcendent imagining. Someone in 2021 who is imagining their dream vacation might do so without consideration of the actual amount of vacation time they have accrued, their actual income, or the actually occurring global pandemic. That's not to say we don't impose *any* constraints in cases of transcendent imagining. For example, when pretending to be pirates, Priya and Penny might retain the constraint of Earth's gravity. It might be important to the game of pretense that they're playing that the other kids (that is, the rival pirate gangs) are not able to float across the playground (the ocean) to the sandbox (the island) where the treasure is buried. In other games of pretense, however, they might release this constraint as well. For example, if they are playing a game of pretense where they are deep space explorers and the playground has become the surface of Jupiter, they might imagine a much heavier gravitational pull. As a general matter, transcendent imaginings are relatively unconstrained, and it's for this reason that they can serve escapist aims.

Matters are different when it comes to instructive imagining. When Dave is trying to figure out whether a particular loveseat will fit the spot he intends to put it in, he has to imagine the loveseat in terms of its actual size and his living room in terms of its actual dimensions. It does him no good to imagine the living room as bigger than it in fact is or the loveseat as smaller than it in fact is; rather, he needs to be constrained by the facts about their actual sizes. When Emily is trying to figure out how Eddie is feeling during his tense exchange with Ellen, she has to imagine his temperament as it actually is. It does her no good to imagine him as having a much more easygoing manner than he in fact has, or as being more inclined to cut Ellen some slack than he in fact is, or as having a better relationship with Ellen than he in fact does. Rather, she needs to be constrained by the facts about his actual personality and past history with Ellen.

Of course, even in instructive imagining, some of the constraints of reality will be removed. That's how we are able to explore what would happen were this or that change to occur. For example, though Dave is imagining his living room exactly as it is in most respects, he is not constrained by the current color of the walls; rather, he changes the color in imagination as he explores the different shades of cream-colored paint. Likewise, he is not constrained by the fact that there's currently a recliner positioned in the living room exactly where he intends the new loveseat to go.

Conversely, just as constraints must sometimes be removed in instructive uses of imagination, constraints must sometimes be imposed in transcendent uses of imagination. This point can be brought out clearly by considering different genres of fiction. A novelist writing historical fiction set during the Civil War will need to constrain their imaginings in a way that a novelist working on science fiction set in the future does not. But even the science fiction novelist will likely need to constrain their imaginings in various ways. As many science fiction authors have observed, constraints play an important role in the development of science fiction plotlines. Gregory Benford, an astrophysicist who has also authored numerous works of science fiction, describes science fiction as "a controlled way to think and dream about the future." Arthur C. Clarke (known for many works, among them the screen-play for *2001: A Space Odyssey*) notes that a science fiction writer "is allowed to invent not-yet-existing technologies, as long as they are plaus-ible" but "must not state as a scientific fact something that is flatly untrue." Moreover, we might naturally differentiate science fiction from the related genre of fantasy precisely in terms of what constraints are operable in each genre. Consider this account of the difference between these two genres offered by John W. Campbell (author and editor of *Astounding Science Fiction*):

> The major distinction between fantasy and science fiction is, simply, that science fiction uses one, or a very, very few new postulates, and develops the rigidly consistent logical consequences of these limited postulates. Fantasy makes its rules as it goes along ... The basic nature of fantasy is "The only rule is, make up a new rule any time you need one!" The basic rule of science fiction is "Set up a basic proposition – then develop its consistent, logical consequences." (Campbell 1966)

As this discussion suggests, authors writing works in one fictional genre must constrain their imagination in different ways from authors writing works in other fictional genres. A similar point will arise for artists as well. While some art strives for realism, some does not. An artist working on a series of realistic paintings set in New York will thus need to constrain their imaginings in a way that an artist working on a series of fantastical paintings set in the lost city of Atlantis will not.

Let's now return to the imaginative activities referenced in our opening vignettes: pretending, decision-making, and understanding the minds of others. The first of these activities falls squarely in the category of transcendent use, while the second and third fall squarely in the category of instructive use. But of course, these are not the only imaginative activities that fall into these categories.

In addition to being put to transcendent use in childhood pretense, imagination is used in a similarly transcendent way by adults when they act on stage or on screen. Daydreaming is another example of imagination's transcendent use, as we saw in the case of Fred earlier. When imagination is invoked in the context of art, literature, or music, this is likely another instance of transcendent use. We have already discussed how imagination is involved in the production of such works, but we should also note the way that imagination is involved in the consumption of such works. A museumgoer uses imagination when viewing the works of art in the gallery. Likewise, a reader uses imagination when reading works of literature – from imagining the faces of the characters and the places they visit to imagining the emotions they experience. Jasper Fforde makes this point (via some remarks by the character Snell) in his novel *The Well of Lost Plots*:

> [R]eading is arguably a far more creative and imaginative process than writing; when the reader creates emotion in their head, or the colors of the sky during the setting sun, or the smell of a warm summer's breeze on their

face, they should reserve as much praise for themselves as they do for the writer – perhaps more. (Fforde 2003, 18)

Many philosophers have thought that imagination is our primary mode of engagement with a fictional text (see, e.g., Walton 1990). For example, upon picking up George Orwell's *1984* and reading the famous first sentence, "It was a bright cold day in April, and the clocks were striking thirteen," we don't form a belief that this is true; rather we imagine it. Interestingly, though this use of imagination is probably best construed as transcendent, it involves much more constraint than other typical transcendent uses of imagination since one typically wants one's imagining to match the text. One is thus constrained by what the author has written.

That said, it's worth noting that readers do on occasion fail to abide by the constraints imposed by the author of the text that they are reading. Sometimes this occurs simply because they choose to ignore such constraints and allow their imaginings to outrun what's being described. But sometimes they actively fight back against the constraints. Consider the phenomenon of imaginative resistance (see, e.g., Gendler 2000). To call upon a famous example by Kendall Walton, suppose a reader of a novel were to encounter the following passage: "In killing her baby, Giselda did the right thing; after all it was a girl" (Walton 1994, 37). Though the reader might be willing to imagine that they're being presented with a world in which people think that female infanticide is morally acceptable, they are likely to resist imagining a fictional world in which it is indeed morally acceptable to commit female infanticide.

Turning from contexts of art and literature to contexts of science or mathematics, we turn from cases where imagination is likely being put to transcendent use to cases where it is likely being put to instructive use.[14] As theoretical physicist Richard Feynman has famously said, a scientist's imagination "is stretched to the utmost, not as in fiction, to imagine things which are not really there, but just to comprehend those things which are there" (Feynman 1965/2017, 127–128). Likewise, when an inventor is trying to develop a new technology, or when a chef is trying to create a new recipe, or when an architect is designing a new building, imagination is also being put to instructive use. Consider the architect John Root, one of the founders of the nineteenth century Chicago-based architectural firm, Burnham and Root. As described by his partner Daniel Burnham, Root had the tremendous ability to imaginatively envision a structure in its entirety: "I've never seen anyone quite like him in this respect. He would grow abstracted and silent, and a faraway look would

---

[14] For discussion of the scientific imagination, see Stuart 2017. For a qualitative study of how scientists actually put imagination to use in their everyday scientific practices, see Stuart 2019.

come into his eyes, and the building was there before him – every stone" (as quoted in Larson 2003).

To give one more example that (for me, at least) is closer to home, when philosophers call upon imagination in the course of developing thought experiments, here too imagination is being put to instructive use.[15] When Derek Parfit asks us to imagine traveling to Mars by way of a *Star Trek*-like teletransporter, our imaginative consideration of the scenario teaches us something about the nature of personal identity (Parfit 1984, 199–201); when Judith Jarvis Thomson asks us to imagine being kidnapped and then hooked up to a famous violinist for nine months in an effort to save his life, we learn something about abortion and the nature of our duties to others (Thomson 1971).

Before closing our discussion of imagination, it will be worth making one last point about these two different uses of imagination, a point that we return to once we turn to a consideration of the relationship between imagination and creativity. In short, there seem to be important connections to creativity in both of these different uses of imagination. Though we intuitively tend to associate creativity with the ability to think outside the box – and thus with the unshackling of constraints – it is not just unconstrained imagining that can be thought of as creative thinking. Just as the children playing pretend and the painters and novelists creating works of art and literature will sometimes be appropriately described as doing something creative, so too the scientists, mathematicians, inventors, and philosophers will sometimes be appropriately described as doing something creative. As we come to understand the nature of creative thinking, we will see how it is involved in both transcendent and instructive contexts of imagining.

3 What Is Creativity?

Intuitively speaking, the essence of creativity seems to lie in originality and novelty. But it doesn't take much reflection to raise the suspicion that more must be required, that not everything that's novel should count as creative. Using my iPhone's predictive text function and choosing the middle word suggested each time, I just produced the following three lines (I hesitate to refer to them as sentences):

> Maybe I should be there by this time and then I can I have a question about the other stuff that we will put on our table

> Thanks again and for the update I am so sorry I didn't think you be a problem until now

> Good luck to your next day and your family

---

[15] For a discussion of thought experiments, see Brown and Fehige 2019.

Each of these lines can plausibly be seen as novel. Certainly I've never produced them before, and I suspect that at least one of the three (if not more) has never been produced before by anyone else either. But I don't feel any temptation to count any of them as creative. As noted by creativity researchers Mark Runco and Garrett Jaeger in arguing that originality alone is not sufficient for creativity: "Originality can be found in the word salad of a psychotic and can be produced by monkeys on word processors" (Runco and Jaeger 2012, 92). This basic point traces back at least to the eighteenth-century work of philosopher Immanuel Kant, who famously noted that there can be "original nonsense" just as much as there can be original works of genius.

Interestingly, we might dispute this Kantian dichotomy. Consider a work such as Lewis Carroll's "Jabberwocky,"[16] a poem that opens as follows:

> 'Twas brillig, and the slithy toves
> Did gyre and gimble in the wabe:
> All mimsy were the borogoves,
> And the mome raths outgrabe.

There's good reason to think that this poem is both nonsense *and* genius. That said, however, there's still an important point in what Kant is saying. On his view, something that's creative must in some way be exemplary, that is, it must serve as a model for others, in addition to being original.

In contemporary philosophy, this Kantian point is often put in terms of value, and there is widespread (though not unanimous) consensus that both of the two features that we've just identified, originality and value, should be included in any adequate definition of creativity. (We'll return to questions raised about the value requirement in Section 3.2.1.) In the empirical literature, this bipartite definition is referred to as *the standard definition of creativity* (Runco and Jaeger 2012, 92).[17] But despite the widespread agreement that both these features are necessary for creativity, there is considerably less agreement about whether they are sufficient for creativity, that is, many scholars argue that the standard definition does not go far enough. Whether anything else is also required – and if so, what – are hotly contested issues.

There are many other hotly contested issues in discussions of creativity as well. What role does luck play in creativity? What is the relationship between creativity and consciousness? Can creativity be learned? We will return to these issues when we discuss the connection between imagination and creativity in

---

[16] www.poetryfoundation.org/poems/42916/jabberwocky

[17] Though as we have seen, philosophers have been giving this sort of definition of creativity at least since Kant, Runco and Jaeger (2012, 94–95) point to Stein (1953) as having given the first unambiguous statement of the standard definition in the empirical literature.

Section 4. First, however, we will discuss creativity itself in more detail. Our discussion has two main aims: (i) to distinguish different kinds of creativity; and (ii) to explore in more detail how creativity can be defined.

3.1 Varieties of Creativity

Just as there are numerous taxonomies of imagination in play in the imagination literature, there are numerous taxonomies of creativity in play in the creativity literature. In what follows we will focus on two such taxonomies. These taxonomies do not compete with one another but rather are best seen as complementary.

3.1.1 Exemplars of Creativity

The first taxonomy that we'll consider aims to distinguish three different kinds of exemplars to which the notion of creativity applies. As in our discussion of imagination, we are helped by consideration of three vignettes:

> *Inspiring Invitee.* A college is looking for an inspiring speaker to give their convocation address. Finally, the selection committee decides to invite an individual known as Indigo who works in technology. "The students will learn so much from Indigo," the chair of the committee concludes. "He's so accomplished and such a creative person."

> *Mathematical Musings.* In math class, Marisol is called to the board to demonstrate homework problem #5. She explains how she tackled the problem and what answer she got. After complimenting her, her teacher notes, "Interesting! You got the same answer that I did, but I've never seen anyone take that approach before. That's a very creative way to solve the problem."

> *Computer Chess.* Camisha, an excellent chess player, is practicing by competing against her favorite computer opponent. The program works by brute force, first exploring the legally available moves in line with a preexisting algorithm that narrows down the possibilities and assigns them various weights, and then choosing the optimal result. At a certain point in the game, Camisha finds herself extremely surprised by the computer's move. "What a creative choice!" she thinks to herself, after working out why the move was advantageous for her computer opponent. "I never would have thought of doing that."

Though each of these vignettes seems to present us with an example of creativity, they each apply the adjective "creative" to a different sort of exemplar. In Inspiring Invitee, what's described as creative is a particular person (in this case, the mononymic Indigo). Call this *person-creativity*. In Mathematical Musings, what's described as creative is a particular process (in this case, a process of mathematical reasoning). Call this *process-creativity*. In Computer Chess, what's described as creative is a particular product (in this case, a chess move). Call this *product-creativity*. Of course, many other kinds of products over and above chess moves will fall under this type of creativity, from musical compositions and works of art, to technological devices and mechanical inventions, to scientific discoveries and philosophical theories. To put it in terms used by Margaret Boden, the products might be either *ideas* or *artifacts* (Boden 1990/2005, 1).

These three kinds of creativity are undoubtedly connected to one another. For example, it might be that creative processes are in general more likely to yield creative products than noncreative processes, and it also might be that what makes a person aptly described as creative is their use of creative processes and/or their success in generating creative products. But the three kinds of creativity do not always go hand in hand, and we might have one without the other. It seems plausible that in Computer Chess, the computer produces the creative move without using a creative method for getting there – so we have product-creativity without process-creativity.[18] In Mathematical Musings, we have the reverse scenario: process-creativity without product-creativity. Marisol is able to come up with the right answer to the problem she was assigned by a creative problem-solving route, but there was nothing especially novel or interesting about the answer itself. As for Inspiring Invitee, we don't know enough about Indigo to know why he's thought of as creative, but this could well be a case where we have person-creativity without process-creativity (perhaps, unbeknownst to the public he's landed on several creative innovations purely by accident) or where we have person-creativity without product-creativity (Indigo might be known for a particularly innovative style of thinking, even though he himself has not put that kind of thinking to work in producing any real output).

Having distinguished these three types of creativity, one might wonder whether one of them is more fundamental than the others. Perhaps unsurprisingly, this is a matter about which there is a fair amount of disagreement. Some theorists argue that person-creativity is the primary kind of creativity (see, e.g., Audi 2018). This way of thinking about creativity aligns nicely with thinking of it as a virtue or character trait (see also Kieran 2014). Other theorists argue that process-creativity is the primary kind of creativity and that creativity applies only (or at least, in the first instance) to mental processes (see, e.g., Gaut 2010; Nanay 2014; Paul and Stokes 2018). Finally other theorists, particularly psychologists and other empirical researchers, see product-creativity as fundamental.

---

[18] As noted by Berys Gaut and Matthew Kieran, "An entirely mechanical search, trial and error procedure leading to a new discovery hardly seems the essence of creativity" (2018, 3).

In fact, expressions of the standard definition of creativity found in the empirical literature are focused on creativity as applied to products.

For our purposes here, we will not need to adjudicate this dispute. There's much of interest to say about all three kinds of creativity, and the discussion of this section will have something to say about each. That said, it's worth noting that it's process-creativity that probably has the most natural connections to imagination. (Of the three kinds of creativity, it's process-creativity that is best captured by the label "creative thinking" used in the title of this Element.) Thus, when we turn to connections between imagination and creativity in Section 4, we will focus primarily on process-creativity.

3.1.2 H-Creativity versus P-Creativity

Poor Elisha Gray. A key player in the development of telegraphic equipment in the 1860s and 1870s, he came up with a viable idea for a telephone transmitter in late 1865. Unfortunately, however, he put off trying to patent his idea for a couple of months. When he finally went to the patent office on February 14, 1876 to file formal notice of his idea, it turned out that Alexander Graham Bell had filed a full patent application earlier that very same day. Though Gray may actually have been the first one to have had the idea for the telephone, Bell is the one credited with its invention (Hounshell 1975).

The story of the invention of the telephone is just one of numerous instances throughout history of near-simultaneous invention of new technology or near-simultaneous development of a new theory. Gottfried Leibniz and Isaac Newton each independently developed the theory of calculus in the late seventeenth century, and although Leibniz published his theory first, it's likely that Newton was the first of the two to come up with the relevant ideas. In the late nineteenth century, several different bacteriologists working independently in different countries invented a kind of culture dish that has come to be known as the Petri dish. Much more recently, the COVID-19 pandemic of 2020 provides us another prominent instance of near-simultaneous invention, when pharmaceutical companies Pfizer and Moderna both developed mRNA vaccines within weeks of one another.

The creation of these COVID-19 vaccines seems a clear example of scientific creativity. But, strictly speaking, only one of them was first. Which one? The answer will be different depending on exactly what criteria we use. For example, although the Pfizer vaccine was the first to be authorized for use, Moderna was actually the first to go into clinical trials.[19] But neither of these milestones seems like the right one to focus on for assessing which was invented

---

[19] See Grady 2020.

first, and we undoubtedly need to go back further in the timeline. Though I haven't been able to ferret out the precise details for when the formula for each vaccine was completed, it's clear that the first clinical batch of the Moderna vaccine was created on February 7, 2020 with the first clinical batch of the Pfizer vaccine coming in March. Given the facts I have, it looks like Moderna probably crossed the finish line first. When the Pfizer vaccine was first synthesized, it was not truly original, for the Moderna vaccine already existed. Does that mean that the Pfizer vaccine and the pharmaceutical scientists who created it should not be described as creative? And likewise for Gray (given that Bell beat him to the finish line), and for Leibniz (assuming that Newton had the ideas first)?

We can best answer this question by introducing an influential distinction made by philosopher Margaret Boden in her seminal work on creativity. Boden distinguishes between what she calls *psychological creativity* (or P-creativity) and *historical creativity* (or H-creativity). Psychological creativity is confined to the context of a particular mind that has the creative idea: "If Mary Smith combines ideas in a way she's never done before, or if she has an idea which she could not have had before, her idea is P-creative – no matter how many people have had the same idea already" (Boden 1990/2005, 43). In contrast, historical creativity is not limited to the context of an individual mind: "The historical sense applies to ideas that are novel with respect to *the whole of human history*. Mary Smith's surprising idea is H-creative only if no one has ever had that idea before her" (Boden 1990/2005, 43).

As described, this distinction seems best understood in terms of product-creativity, with Mary Smith's creative idea being the product in question. But it can be extended to person-creativity and process-creativity as well. A person can be described as P-creative in virtue of producing a prodigious number of P-creative products, and they can be likewise described as H-creative in virtue of producing a prodigious number of H-creative products. A process can be described as P-creative in virtue of its success as leading to P-creative products, and it can be likewise described as H-creative in virtue of its success at leading to H-creative products. Of course, we might also think that a process can be described as P-creative or H-creative nonderivatively. For example, we might consider a process that itself exhibits novelty and value to be P-creative or H-creative in virtue of these aspects of the process itself.

So what does this tell us about how we should assess creativity in the cases of simultaneous invention we were considering? Assuming that calculus was really an independent discovery by both Leibniz and Newton, and that neither had access to the work of the other, then in each case the discovery can be described as P-creative, though only the one that came historically first would have a claim to H-creativity. And the same goes for the invention of the telephone, the Petri dish, and the COVID-19 vaccine. Of course, it is often hard to assess which independent discovery of an idea was genuinely first. As Boden notes:

> H-creativity is something about which we are often mistaken. Historians of science and art are constantly discovering cases in which other people, even in other periods, have had an idea popularly attributed to some national or international hero. (1994, 76)

In fact, this is likely the case with respect to the discovery of calculus. Some mathematicians now believe that the real discovery of calculus predates Leibniz and Newton by more than two centuries and came via the work of the Kerala school, a group of mathematicians working in India in the fourteenth century.[20] If this account of the discovery of calculus is correct, then we're mistaken to describe either Leibniz's or Newton's discovery of calculus as H-creative. Still, the work by the Kerala mathematicians does not show that we're mistaken in attributing P-creativity to both Leibniz and Newton.

Though the calculus case shows that we can have P-creativity without H-creativity, we should make explicit that we cannot have H-creativity without P-creativity. If something is genuinely new to the world, then it must also have been genuinely new to the mind who created it. P-creativity is the more fundamental notion of the two, and for that reason it will be our focus in what follows. Focusing on P-creativity also allows us to forestall a worry that is sometimes raised about novelty, namely, a worry that achieving novelty is virtually impossible, if not impossible. This kind of worry has biblical roots; as written in *Ecclesiastes* 1:9, "What has been will be again, what has been done will be done again; there is nothing new under the sun." But even if nothing can be new to the earth, it can still be new to the psychology of an individual mind.

3.2 Defining Creativity

With these two crosscutting taxonomies of creativity before us, we can now return to the question of how creativity should be defined. Recall the standard definition of creativity that we encountered earlier: Creativity involves both novelty and value. If there's one issue about creativity that is entirely without dispute, it concerns the first of these two elements. There's no question that creativity involves novelty. Our discussion of H-creativity versus P-creativity helps us to pin down what exactly is meant by these notions. But what about

---

[20] For discussion, see Almeida and Joseph 2004.

value? And are there other requirements that should be added to the standard definition? In this section, we tackle each of these questions in turn.

3.2.1 The Value Requirement

At the start of our discussion of creativity, I noted that there was widespread agreement that both novelty and value were required for creativity (in either the sense of P-creativity or H-creativity), but I also noted that this agreement was not unanimous. Why have some philosophers rejected the value requirement on creativity?

On first thought, one might feel tempted to reject the value requirement because it seems too demanding. Consider the drawings of a young child. While these drawings might be treasured and even framed by adoring parents, they're unlikely to sell for much (or even at all) on eBay or anywhere else, nor is anyone other than the parents and possibly the grandparents likely to have any interest in displaying them. Insofar as at least some of these drawings seem rightly judged to be creative, requiring that something be valuable for it to count as creative looks to be problematic. But here it's important to note that philosophers who include the value requirement in their definition of creativity tend to have a deflationary sense of value in mind. For something to meet the value requirement, it need not have *great* value, either monetary or otherwise. Rather, it's enough that it positively impacts the world in some way, even if that impact is an extremely minimal one.

But even if this worry about the value requirement can be easily dismissed, there are other worries that have had more traction. One such worry concerns the uninformativeness of this requirement. As Dustin Stokes has argued, the inclusion of a value criterion in a theory of creativity fails to add any explanatory value to that theory. What we need to know is not *that* something is valued but *why* it is valued. He defends this claim by way of an analogy. Suppose you wanted to better understand the nature of a carburetor. Being told that a carburetor is a very valuable part of an internal combustion engine provides you with no insight into what a carburetor is or what it does. Likewise, says Stokes, being told that creative things are valuable provides you with no insight into what creativity is. It tells you nothing about *why* creative products or processes are valuable. Stokes thus concludes that we would be better off in our efforts to analyze creativity were we simply "to grant that creative things are valuable, and then attempt to identify reasons for thinking they are valuable – conditions on creative thought and behaviour" (Stokes 2011, 676). Note, however, that even if this line of reasoning were correct, it would not suggest that we're mistaken in thinking that value is necessary for something to be creative. Being told that a triangle is a three-sided closed figure might not give you any deep insight into what a triangle is, but being three-sided is nonetheless a component of any adequate analysis of triangularity; likewise, being told that something is valuable might not give you any deep insight into why it is creative, but being valuable might nonetheless be a component of any adequate analysis of creativity.

A different reason offered to worry about the value requirement stems from the fact that creativity might arise in connection with projects that lack value, even in the deflationary sense of value with which we've been operating. In defense of this claim, Alison Hills and Alexander Bird ask us to consider the development of novel and ingenious scientific theories that prove to be false. In some cases, a false theory might gain a kind of indirect value by furthering scientific progress. Even though the theory might not even be approximately true, it might be productive in leading to a deeper understanding of the phenomenon to be explained. But this won't always be the case. Sometimes, a false theory ends up proving entirely unhelpful. It doesn't lead to any further understanding or scientific progress. This lack of productivity, however, does not itself show that the theory cannot be appropriately described as creative. As an example, Hills and Bird point to creationism: "Creationist ideas, such as special creation, may be creative attempts to find a theory that reconciles creationist precepts with the evidence. But they are scientifically worthless" (Hills and Bird 2018, 98). This is likewise true for attempted inventions that were spectacular failures, such as the time machine built by Gordon Earl Adams in the late 1920s. The *New York Times* describes the machine as having "dozens of flywheels, some perhaps weighing several tons and looking as if they could spin so fast that they would set off powerful electrical charges into the atmosphere."[21] Though Adams' invention didn't work, and though it didn't yield any important insights toward future invention, we might still be inclined to think of it as a *creative* failure.

If these examples are accepted, then creativity can be associated with products that lack value. But Hills and Bird want to go one step further: Some creative projects might not just lack positive value but actually have negative value. Consider a serial killer who employs novel and ingenious ways of murdering victims or a torturer who develops novel and ingenious ways of causing pain.[22] In each case, it seems apt to describe the methods as creative, but in using this description, we do not imply that they are valuable. As Hills and Bird note, "There is no contradiction in the idea that creativity can be put to terrible ends" (Hills and Bird 2018, 97). Paisley Livingston makes a similar point, noting that it is "not contradictory to speak of 'bad creativity'" (Livingston 2018).

---

[21] See Bradley 2014.

[22] For other examples of this sort, see Rogers 1954.

One might try to extrapolate a further moral from this discussion by noting that the inclusion of a value criterion in the definition of creativity improperly introduces a subjective element to the notion of creativity. Carl Rogers makes this kind of argument, pointing to the fact that the creative discoveries of scientists such as Galileo and Copernicus were once regarded as blasphemous and wicked but are now no longer viewed in that way. In his view, this offers good reason to jettison the value requirement: "We do not want to cloud our definition with terms which rest in subjectivity" (Rogers 1954, 251). But one needn't adopt a subjectivist understanding of value to be moved by the examples of creativity that are value-neutral or have disvalue. In offering their examples of bad creativity, philosophers such as Hills and Bird or Livingston have an objective understanding of value in mind.

Responding to these kinds of examples, some philosophers have argued that the notion of value that factors in definitions of creativity needs to be understood in a more nuanced way. We might, for example, focus on instrumental value (see Livingston 2018). The torturer's novel methods of inflicting pain don't have any intrinsic value, but because they serve the torturer's ends, they have instrumental value. But other defenders of the value requirement simply stick to their guns and deny that novel torture methods should be seen as creative. Boden, for example, argues that to call someone or something creative is not merely to give a description but to "express approval or respect." Insofar as we don't want to express approval or respect for the novel torture methods (or for the torturer employing them), Boden suggests that we should retain the value requirement on creativity and maintain our initial judgment that the torture methods lack value. In a similar vein, David Novitz suggests that such methods should not be seen as genuinely creative but rather as ingenious, or "ingeniously destructive" (Novitz 1999, 78).

3.2.2 Other Criteria

Suppose that we are convinced that creativity requires both novelty and value. We might still wonder whether it requires anything else in addition. Many philosophers have argued that it does, and they have proposed various other conditions that they claim should be added to the novelty and value conditions (or, in some cases, that they claim should replace them). We will focus on two such conditions that have been especially prominent in discussions of creativity, surprisingness and agency.[23] As these conditions are understood:

---

[23] To give a couple of examples of other conditions that appear in the literature: Maria Kronfelder (2009) argues that creativity involves originality (where this does not seem to be the same notion as novelty) and spontaneity (where this involves independence from intentional control).

- *Surprisingness*. For something to be creative it must be surprising.
- *Agency*. For something to be creative it must be the result of intentional agency.

Let's take these one at a time.

The requirement that something be surprising in order for it to be judged creative has been forcefully defended by Boden. Though surprisingness relates to novelty, it is meant to be a different notion; for Boden, not everything that is novel is surprising. In her view, surprise might be generated in several different ways. Sometimes a given product counts as surprising because it is an unusual or unexpected combination. This is what Boden calls *combinatorial creativity*. In James Cameron's movie *Avatar* (2009), we see an instance of combinatorial creativity in the depiction of the Na'vi. A novel blend of human body shape with animal features and different color, the Na'vi are an alien species of blue humanoids with pointy ears and tails. For a slightly different kind of combinatorial creativity, consider Julie Taymor's 2010 version of *The Tempest*. In reimagining this Shakespearean play on screen, she transformed the lead role from the male Prospero to a female Prospera (played by Helen Mirren). This casting choice was both surprising and effective. As noted by *New York Times* critic A.O. Scott:

> When the character is a woman, a central relationship in the play, between the magician and her doted-on child, Miranda, sheds some of its traditional, patriarchal dynamic. Instead, a mother-daughter bond fraught with envy, protectiveness and identification blossoms into something newly rich and strange.

For Boden, however, we can achieve a deeper form of surprise when we move beyond combinatorial creativity to either what we call *exploratory creativity* or what she calls *transformational creativity*.[24] Both of these kinds of creativity can be understood in terms of the notion of conceptual frameworks or spaces. Consider the discovery of elements such as Gallium (found in 1875) and Germanium (found in 1886), or the scientific synthesis of elements that do not occur naturally on Earth such as Technetium (synthesized in 1937). The surprise of these discoveries did not result from new combinations of old ideas but rather from new explorations in conceptual space, in this case the conceptual space developed by Russian chemist Dmitri Mendeleev who mapped out the periodic table in the late 1860s. These discoveries are thus examples of exploratory creativity.

---

[24] Though Boden's threefold distinction between combinatorial, exploratory, and transformational creativity has been highly influential, for an argument against it, see Novitz 1999. Novitz also argues that deep surprise can come without transformational creativity in Boden's sense.

But now consider cases where one does not simply explore a preexisting conceptual space but instead transforms or transcends it. Sometimes this might occur by dropping a constraint that had previously seemed necessary, as when non-Euclidean geometry was developed by dropping Euclid's fifth postulate, the parallel postulate. Other times it might occur by way of dramatic and deep reconceptualization, so profound that previous theory is entirely displaced, as when Einstein developed his theories of relativity. These instances of transformational creativity produce an especially deep form of surprise. In fact, in Boden's view the surprise generated by instances of transformational creativity is often so deep that the novel developments seem not just improbable but impossible.

As defined by Boden, surprisingness seems to apply primarily to product-creativity. Perhaps it could be extended to process-creativity by understanding the relevant creative processes as combinatorial, exploratory, or transformational. Insofar as it could be extended to person-creativity, this would be in a derivative sense in which the surprisingness element of person-creativity gets defined in terms of the surprisingness element of product-creativity. Someone who has person-creativity satisfies the surprisingness requirement insofar as their creative outputs are surprising.

Let's focus our evaluation of the surprisingness requirement on consideration of product-creativity. Though it seems initially plausible that many creative products generate surprise, one might worry that this need not be true for *all* creative products. Apparent counterexamples are especially easy to find in instances of P-creativity without H-creativity. When children "discover" that a lemon can produce electricity, or that heavier objects do not fall faster than lighter objects (they might do a bottle drop experiment, with two water bottles of the same size, one full of water and one only half full), their teacher is unlikely to be surprised, but the discovery seems P-creative nonetheless.[25] Of course, in such a case the children themselves might be surprised by their discovery, so perhaps we might take the requirement to relate to surprisingness *to the creator* rather than to others. But this suggestion proves problematic as well. In some cases, a creator might have been working on a given project for so long, and might have pictured the result so clearly in their mind, that they view the creative output as inevitable rather than as surprising.

One way to address this concern is to move away from understanding surprise in a phenomenological way, that is, from understanding it in terms of our own experience or reaction. For the requirement to still be a substantive

---

[25] Descriptions of these experiments, and instructions for how to conduct them, are easily found on the web.

requirement, however, we would have to do so in a way that maintains a distinction between surprisingness and novelty, and it's not clear exactly how this can be done. As Berys Gaut notes, the surprisingness requirement might be best understood as simply a modification of the novelty requirement, one that specifies the salient sense of novelty needed for creativity (2010, 1039). Owing to considerations like these, the surprisingness requirement has not been widely adopted.

Like the surprisingness requirement, the agency requirement seems best understood as applying in the first instance to product-creativity. According to this requirement, in order for a given product to count as creative it must have been produced by an agent. To use one of Gaut's examples, consider an "elegant and distinct canopy of leaves" produced by a tree (2018, 129). The canopy might reasonably be described as both new and valuable. Absent the agency requirement, then, such a canopy would fall under our definition of product-creativity, and the tree that produced it would fall under our definition of person-creativity. Gaut points to other similar examples as well, such as a beautiful new pearl produced by an oyster or a unique and valuable diamond produced by certain tectonic movements of the earth. On Gaut's view, we can best explain why these products and their creators should not be classified as creative by adopting an account of creativity that builds in a requirement of agency.

In fact, Gaut wants to go one step further, requiring not only agency but *intentional* agency. Not every new and valuable creation by an agent is done intentionally. Sometimes it is simply a lucky accident. Suppose a clueless teenager wearing AirPods knocks over the ketchup bottle, steps in the spilled condiment, and then proceeds to track it all around the kitchen while putting together an after-school snack. All of this happens without the teenager even noticing it. And now suppose that the footprints on the floor end up creating a visually attractive and unusual pattern, so much so that when the teenager's mother posts a picture of it on Instagram in an attempt to garner sympathy for her parenting woes, many of her followers take it to be a work of art. Alternatively, for a real-life case, consider Charles Goodyear's attempts to vulcanize rubber, that is, to find a way to make the rubber durable enough for use in industrial contexts. Though various treatments were available to transform rubber from its original sap-like form to something malleable, it would still become sticky when hot and brittle when cold. Goodyear's efforts to find a solution were wide-ranging and one might even say bizarre. He tried mixing rubber with a great variety of substances including witch hazel, magnesia, castor oil, acids, and even cream cheese. Success came only as a result of a lucky accident. One day when he was working with a mixture of rubber and sulfur, it inadvertently came into contact with a hot stove, and he realized that he had found what he was looking for.[26]

Goodyear's vulcanization technique was certainly novel and valuable, and the teenager's ketchup painting might well be art, but should they be described as creative? Insofar as our intuitions here suggest a negative answer to the question, we can see why it's plausible to qualify the agency requirement in terms of intentional agency. But some might question whether even the qualification in terms of intentionality is enough. While the requirement that the agency in question be intentional gets around the accidental cases just discussed, there are other cases for which even this qualifier might not be enough. Consider a case where someone makes an original and valuable work of art by way of a "paint-by-numbers" technique. Denying that this case counts as an instance of creativity, Gaut notes that the problem arises from the fact that "she is following exactly specified rules, which leave no room for individual judgement" (2010, 1040; see also Kronfelder 2009). In an attempt to explicate the way in which intentional agency must be required for creativity, he goes on to suggest that:

> The kinds of actions that are creative are ones that exhibit at least a relevant purpose (in not being purely accidental), some degree of understanding (not using merely mechanical search procedures), a degree of judgement (in how to apply a rule, if a rule is involved) and an evaluative ability directed to the task at hand. As shorthand for these features, we can say that creative actions must exhibit *flair*. (2010, 140–141)

Note that here we seem to have moved from a discussion of product-creativity to process-creativity.

Should the flair requirement, or some other version of the agency requirement, be added to the standard definition of creativity? In addition to the kinds of cases just discussed, we can briefly note two further considerations in favor of some such requirement. First, recall the fact, noted earlier, that a description of something as creative seems to involve a judgment of approval or respect. Creative things are judged worthy of praise (see Stokes 2011). These kinds of judgments might seem to presuppose agency. Just as good deeds done unintentionally don't merit respect or praise, original and valuable deeds done unintentionally also don't merit respect or praise. Second, given that many philosophers want to draw a connection between imagination and creativity, an agency requirement proves useful in providing an explanation of the connection. The more we see these two topics as connected, then, the more we might be inclined toward accepting this kind of requirement.

---

[26] The example of Goodyear is also found in Novitz 1999, Nanay 2014, and Gaut 2010.

Interestingly, acceptance of the agency requirement forces us to rethink one of our initial vignettes about creativity, namely, Computer Chess. Though the chess program produces a move that surprises its human opponent Camisha, and though the move is both original and valuable, it seems implausible that the computer program is an intentional agent (and it's likewise implausible that its computational processes are the result of intentional agency). The problem is not limited to chess programs. As we will see in our discussion of machine creativity and imagination in Section 5, there is a significant tension between accepting the agency requirement and recognizing machines and machine processes as creative.

4 How Are Imagination and Creativity Related?

In ordinary discourse, the words "imagination" and "creativity" are often used interchangeably. Children who engage in elaborate games of pretense or who draw fantastical scenes might naturally be described both as having a great imagination and as being very creative, and likewise for scientists who come up with pathbreaking new theories or architects who come up with innovative designs. Given the near-synonymy of the notions, one might be tempted to conclude that there's no difference between imagination and creativity, that is, that they should be identified with one another.[27] To my mind, this would be a mistake. Our discussion thus far has already provided some reasons to push back against this, not least of which is the simple point that "imagination" and "creativity" seem to be referring to different kinds of things. While imagination is a mental activity, creativity is not. Though it can be a feature of mental activity – as is the case when we're focused on process-creativity – it can also be a feature of persons and products.[28] That said, even if we reject the *identification* of imagination with creativity, there does seem to be something importantly right about the idea that creativity and imagination are tightly connected. As Peter Langland-Hassan has noted, it's simply platitudinous that being creative requires you to have a good imagination: "There are no creative geniuses lacking in imagination; and there are no creative acts in which the creator's imaginativeness played no role" (2020, 263).

---

[27] Indeed, we sometimes encounter this view (or something very much like it) in the philosophical literature, e.g., James Grant (2018, 333) claims that creativity is the same thing as imaginativeness.

[28] One might try to get around this point by limiting one's attention to creative thinking more specifically rather than creativity more broadly. Is "creative thinking" just another way to refer to exercises of imagination? In my view, even this conclusion is mistaken. This is particularly apparent if we're operating with an imagery-based account of imagination, as one might engage in creative thinking without utilizing mental images. But we needn't adopt this kind of account to make the point; see the discussion of *Mathematical Musings* below.

What, exactly, is the nature of this connection? Section 4.1 takes up this question in some detail. In Section 4.2, we turn to an important aspect of both imagination and creativity that undergirds their connection, namely, that they can both be understood within a skills-based framework.

4.1 The Nature of the Relation

When we think about the examples of creativity that we've discussed throughout this Element, many of them seem likely to have involved exercises of imagination. Indeed, it seems plausible that exercises of imagination are typically involved in any case where creativity is being exhibited. Can we go one step further here? That is, even if creativity and imagination are not the same thing, would it be reasonable to claim that exercises of imagination are *always* involved in cases where creativity is being exhibited? And, conversely, is creativity *always* exhibited when one's imagination is being exercised?

4.1.1 Three Claims

In thinking about these questions, it will be helpful to introduce a distinction often made in philosophy between necessary and sufficient conditions. When one phenomenon X is *sufficient* for another phenomenon Y, the existence or occurrence of X will guarantee the existence or occurrence of Y. Y might be possible without X, but if X occurs, Y must also occur – X guarantees it. For example, being a member of the United States House of Representatives is sufficient for being a member of the United States Congress. If you're a member of the House of Representatives, this guarantees that you're a member of Congress. But note that while membership in the House of Representatives is sufficient for membership in Congress, it is not necessary for being a member of the Congress. You would also be a member of the US Congress if you are a Senator. When one phenomenon X is *necessary* for another phenomenon Y, the existence or occurrence of Y is not possible without the existence or occurrence of X. X might be possible without Y, but if Y occurs, X must also occur – Y requires it. For example, being at least thirty-five years old is necessary for being president of the United States. If you're president of the United States, then you must be at least thirty-five years old; being president requires that you be at least that age. But, as should be obvious, being at least thirty-five years old is not sufficient for being president of the United States. At the time of this writing in 2021, people such as William Shatner (age ninety) and Beyoncé (age forty) and Aziz Ansari (age thirty-eight) all meet this condition, but none of them is president of the United States.

Though we've just considered one condition that was sufficient for a given phenomenon without being necessary for it, and one that was necessary for a given phenomenon without being sufficient for it, sometimes one condition is both necessary and sufficient for a given phenomenon. For example, for a closed figure to have exactly three interior angles, it is both necessary and sufficient that it has exactly three sides. Of course, that's not to say that the property of triangularity is the very same property as the property of having three sides. Even when one phenomenon is both necessary and sufficient for another, it does not mean that the two phenomena are the same. To use another example that has been frequently invoked by philosophers, it turns out that having a heart is both a necessary and a sufficient condition for having a kidney; circulatory systems and waste-removal systems go hand in hand. But having a heart is not the very same thing as having a kidney.

With this distinction between necessary and sufficient conditions in place, we can thus distinguish three different claims about the relationship between imagination and creativity:

> *The necessity claim*: Imagination is necessary for creativity.
> *The sufficiency claim*: Imagination is sufficient for creativity.
> *The necessity+sufficiency* claim: Imagination is both necessary
>   and sufficient for creativity.

All three of these claims appear in the philosophical literature, though the first is the most common. For example, Robert Audi demonstrates his endorsement of the necessity claim when he notes that imagination is the "chief constituent" of creativity (2018, 27), as do Hills and Bird when they define creativity as being "generated through use of imagination" (2018, 95; see also Stokes 2014).[29] Charles Taliaferro and Meredith Varie also endorse (or at least come near to endorsing) the necessity claim when they note that "in most cases of when a person is creative, we assume or recognize that the person exercised her imagination in the creative act or process" (2018, 141). Indeed, given that they see the concept of creativity as "very close" to the concept of imagination, it looks like they might well endorse the necessity+sufficiency claim as well.

The sufficiency claim might be especially attractive when we think about how the novelty requirement on creativity might be satisfied. Recall the characterization of imagination that we encountered at the start of this Element: When we imagine, we represent a scenario without aiming at things as they actually, presently, and subjectively are. In doing so, we achieve a departure from reality, and we thus achieve the kind of novelty that creativity requires.

---

[29] We also find endorsement of the necessity claim in the psychological literature, as in the claim "Without imagination, there can be no creativity" (Gottlieb et al. 2019, 709).

If this line of reasoning is right, and if the imagining also produced something of value, then imagination would be sufficient for creativity.

In fact, a similar line of reasoning might be used to defend the necessity claim as well. A representation of things as they actually are, as happens with belief, would not enable one to achieve novelty. Rather, it's only by departing from things as they actually are that we are able to meet the novelty requirement on creativity. Thus, it looks like imagination is not only sufficient to bring that about, but it is also required. If this is right, and we have reason to believe both the necessity and the sufficiency claims, then we'd also have reason to believe the necessity+sufficiency third claim.

The necessity claim might also be especially attractive to someone who endorses the agency condition, that is, someone who thinks that creativity must be at least partly defined in terms of agency. As we saw earlier in Section 2.1.2, imagination is a voluntary activity. In being the product of one's will, an exercise of imagination will be a product of one's agency. Thus, if agency is required for creativity, we might think that the involvement of imagination is the most natural way to meet that requirement. Indeed, one might be hard-pressed to see how else that requirement could be met.

While there are thus good reasons to endorse both the necessity and the sufficiency claims (and hence the necessity+sufficiency claim as well), there are also good reasons to worry about each of them. To see what's wrong with the sufficiency claim, it will be helpful to return to our opening vignettes involving imagination. Recall Penny and Priya, who are engaged in an elaborate game of pretense on the playground. When they pretend to be pirates, they are exercising their imagination but they are not doing anything especially novel. Children have been pretending to be pirates for generations. Of course, this only shows that they're not doing anything that's H-creative, but let's suppose that this is a regular game of theirs, something that they've played many times before on the playground. Even if the game counted as P-creative the very first time they played, it no longer does. Since Penny and Priya are engaged in imaginative acts without doing anything creative, the sufficiency claim must be false. And the example of Penny and Priya is not the only one that we could have called upon to show this. When Dave calls upon his imagination in the service of his redecorating project, he need not be doing anything novel.

Even more compelling cases of imagination without creativity can be found if we move beyond our opening vignettes. Consider, for example, someone who is having trouble falling asleep. Worrying about the trip they are taking the next day, they keep imagining a plane crash, again and again and again. This imagining doesn't help to calm their nerves, or make them sleepier, and it doesn't seem to have any other value either. Moreover, it also lacks novelty.

As these various examples show, then, exercising one's imagination is not sufficient for creativity. To see what's wrong with the necessity claim, we can return to our vignettes about creativity. Recall Marisol, whose solution to one of her math homework problems was described as creative. There's no special reason to think that Marisol called upon her imagination to arrive at this solution. Fleshing out the case further, we might note that the steps that she took to work her way through the problem seemed completely natural and even automatic to her. She never even had to pause to consider what to do next. And she did not produce any imagery – visual or otherwise. In short, she took an unusual pathway through the various mathematical rules that had been previously taught to her, but she needn't have used her imagination to find that pathway. Insofar as this mathematical process was novel and valuable, as her teacher seemed to think, we would have a case of creativity without imagination. The necessity claim must thus be false; exercising one's imagination is not necessary for creativity.[30]

As should be clear, any counterexamples to the sufficiency and the necessity claims will also serve as counterexamples to the necessity+sufficiency claim. So all three of the claims we have been considering in this section should be rejected. But that said, the problems raised for these claims do nothing to undercut the general sense that imagination and creativity are connected to one another. The problem with these claims is not their attempt to link imagination and creativity but rather their attempt to cast the link as stronger than it in fact is. A more plausible treatment of the connection sees imagination and creativity as frequently or even typically going together, with imagination seen as a primary (or *the* primary) means of achieving creativity even though there might be other means as well.

And in fact, though many articulations of the link between imagination and creativity found in the literature seem to be stated more strongly than is warranted, they can still provide us with insight about the nature of the connection, that is, about how and why imagination is so especially well suited for bringing about creativity. Stokes' work proves especially helpful in this regard. On Stokes' view, creativity requires cognitive manipulation, where cognitive manipulation "typically involves voluntarily thinking about the contents of some conceptual space in non-truth bound ways" (Stokes 2014, 171).

---

[30] Currie and Ravenscroft distinguish two kinds of imagination: recreative imagination, which they describe as the capacity for perspective-shifting, and creative imagination, which involves "the kind of imaginative 'leap' that leads to the creation of something valuable in art, science, or practical life." Their discussion of why recreative imagination is not necessary for what they call creative imagination can be seen as providing support for the claim that imagination is not necessary for creativity (2002, 9–11).

This understanding of creativity fits nicely with Boden's tripartite distinction between combinatorial, exploratory, and transformational creativity that we discussed earlier. We see the centrality of cognitive manipulation in all three of these kinds of creativity, whether it is combining ideas in a new way, exploring the boundaries of a conceptual space, or attempting to move beyond an existing conceptual space.

Stokes then argues that imagination is exactly the right kind of mental exercise for this type of cognitive manipulation. His argument relies on the kinds of features of imagination that we have been discussing: they need not aim at the truth, they are not world-sensitive, and they are also voluntary. Stokes also notes that imagination has the kinds of connections to affect and motivation that one sees in the kind of cognitive activity underlying creativity. For all these reasons, then, he considers imagination to be "the best candidate for serving the cognitive manipulation role" (Stokes 2014, 171; for a similar account, see Gaut 2010).

We might further support Stokes' conclusion by noting that imagination is particularly well positioned to combine ideas in new ways as required for combinatorial creativity (and as useful, if not required, for exploratory and transformational creativity as well); in fact, one might even think combinatorial power is at the very core of imaginative activities. As psychologist Lev Vygotsky has put it, the operation of imagination "depends on combinatorial abilities and practice in exercising them" (1967/2004, 29). David Hume provides us with some further insight into these abilities when he notes that imagination – the "creative power of mind" – consists in "compounding, transposing, augmenting, or diminishing the materials afforded us by the senses and experience" (1777/1977, 11). Likewise, Thomas Nagel notes that imagining proceeds by way of a combination of additions, subtractions, and modifications of one's own prior experiences (1974, 439).

Before moving on, it's also worth noting a further element in Stokes' discussion of imagination's role in creativity. On Stokes' view, imagination involves two different and contrasting aspects: *cognitive playfulness* and *cognitive workfulness*. On the one hand, imagination allows for playful fun and amusement; on the other hand, it can do a lot of important work for us, with imaginative states playing a "rigorous and purposive role in human cognition." Stokes' differentiation of these two features connects to our earlier discussion of the aims of imagining and, in particular, of the transcendent and instructive uses to which imagination can be put. In a further effort to clarify the nature of the relation between imagination and creativity, we will now turn to the question of how these different uses of imagination come into play in the connection between imagination and creativity.

4.1.2 Creativity, Imagination, and Constraint

As we have seen, examples of creativity span a wide range of domains. Much of the philosophical work on creativity focuses mainly on the broad domains of science and art (including not only visual art but also music, poetry, and literature), but there has also been philosophical work on creativity in the context of mathematics (Wenzel 2018), philosophy (Hájek 2018), and morality (Mulgan 2018).[31] For our purposes, though, the examples of science and art prove particularly useful, as they present us with a particularly sharp contrast in the way that creativity manifests. In fact, given this sharp contrast, one might be skeptical that creativity can really be found in both domains. Given the drastically different aims in play in these two different domains, it's hard to see how one and the same phenomenon could really be at work in both of them. This was Kant's view, for example. Having argued in his *Critique of Judgment* that creative genius manifests in the fine arts, Kant rejected the idea that it can manifest in science. Rather, scientists operate in a domain of fact and logic where imagination cannot be given free rein.

Though I don't think we should fully accept the Kantian picture of scientific creativity, these points do help to flesh out the contrast between artistic creativity and scientific creativity, and they also help us to see that this contrast maps roughly onto the distinction between transcendent and instructive imagining. Recall that transcendent imagining functions to enable an imaginer to transcend or escape the reality in which they live, while instructive imagining functions to enable an imaginer to learn about the reality in which they live. As a general matter, creativity in the domain of art seems to rely principally on transcendent uses of imagination, while creativity in the domain of science seems to rely principally on instructive uses of imagining.

For the purpose of the discussion in this subsection, let's set aside considerations relating to the value and agency requirements and focus our attention on the novelty requirement. The achievement of novelty in the domains of both art and science can be understood in terms of the notion of imaginative constraints introduced earlier in Section 2.2. As we noted, while transcendent uses of imagination tend to involve the loosening or removal of constraints, instructive uses of imagination tend to involve the imposition of constraints. But as we also noted, there is often a push and pull between the two, and part of what's involved in putting imagination to good use relative to a given purpose is

---

[31] Outside of the Western philosophical tradition, examples of creativity come from a much broader conception of art, including calligraphy and sword making among many others. For more examples of domains of creativity recognized and valued in non-Western civilizations, see Simonton 2019.

achieving exactly the right balance between releasing and imposing constraints. Indeed, as Boden has noted, constraints should not be seen as opposed to creativity but rather as making creativity possible: "To throw away all constraints would be to destroy the capacity for creative thinking" (1994, 79). Absent any constraint, one has pure randomness, and as Boden notes, random processes alone are unlikely to generate anything interesting and valuable. I recently heard novelist Zadie Smith make a similar point when talking about how she came to write her first play, *The Wife of Willesden*, a twenty-first century reimagining of the Wife of Bath's tale. Like all of the stories in Geoffrey Chaucer's *The Canterbury Tales*, the Wife of Bath's tale is written in rhyming couplets, and so when Smith committed to the play, she also committed herself to writing in that style. In carrying out this daunting task, she noted that this commitment ended up helping rather than hindering her creative process: "Restriction is a very useful thing."[32]

To better understand the relevant push and pull between imposing and releasing constraints, let's consider examples of scientific discovery. Many of these involve instances of exploratory or transformational creativity in Boden's sense. These kinds of creative endeavors are relative to a given conceptual framework, and to operate within that framework, an individual must impose certain constraints on their imagining. Absent these constraints, imaginative explorations will not be able to teach an imaginer anything about the world represented by that conceptual space. But, while the imposition of constraints will be crucial, in these kinds of instructive imaginings, the individual might be able to achieve a greater understanding of the contours of the conceptual space by loosening some of the standard constraints. In some cases, this might be the most productive route to creative discoveries within the conceptual space. Moreover, it might also be that once an individual has loosened some of the constraints imposed by the framework, they are able to move beyond it and transform the conceptual space in such a way that novel ideas can be generated.

Consider, for example, Einstein's famous thought experiment in which he imagined himself traveling at the speed of light alongside a second beam of light traveling in the same direction. This thought experiment revealed problems with Maxwell's theory of electrodynamics and, in particular, with the idea that space is filled with a substance ("luminiferous ether") that serves as a medium for the propagation of light. In performing the thought experiment, Einstein asked himself what that second beam of light looked like from his perspective, and this ultimately led him to the postulation of special relativity. Postulating this thought experiment requires

---

[32] These remarks came during a presentation at Claremont McKenna College in November 2021.

abiding by various constraints having to do with gravity and the speed of light. But it also involves the loosening of other constraints, most importantly, constraints arising from the postulation of the luminiferous ether. Moreover, as suggested by Michael Stuart, engaging in the thought experiment requires one to loosen many other constraints as well. To give just two examples, (1) traveling at the speed of light would actually cause one to explode, so one has to relinquish certain constraints governing how human bodies operate at that speed; and (2) human eyes don't see lightwaves (or at least, we don't directly see them as lightwaves), so one has to relinquish certain constraints about how the human visual system works (Stuart 2020, 974–975).

In thinking about this push and pull between imposing and releasing constraints, it may help to consider two overarching constraints that I have proposed we can see at work in instructive uses of imagination. First is what I call *the reality constraint*. When an individual is guided by the reality constraint, they constrain their imagining so that it captures the world as it is (or, at least, as they believe it to be). Second is what I call *the change constraint*. Often, one's imaginative projects will require imagining a change to the world as it is (or as one believes it to be). When an individual is guided by the change constraint, any time they imagine such a change to the world as it is, they are guided by the logical consequences of that change (Kind 2016). Of course, individuals are not perfect in abiding by these constraints. But as a general matter, the more that imaginings are suitably in line with them, the more the imaginings can teach, and the more that the imaginings can lead to novel ideas that will prove genuinely valuable.

The importance of the reality and change constraints dramatically recedes when we turn from instructive imaginings to transcendent imaginings and, relatedly, from scientific creativity to artistic creativity. The creativity of Picasso's cubist paintings, for example, stems more from the release of constraints than from the imposition of them. Picasso's cubist paintings of human faces bear some resemblance to actual faces in that they depict two eyes, a nose, and a mouth. But beyond that, the paintings are generally not at all constrained by how faces actually look – whether in terms of color, shape, proportion, or location of the facial features. Moreover, the changes to the faces do not seem accurately represented as the logical progression of consequences from a single change. They are far too varied (and, one might say, far too illogical) to be grouped together in that way.

It should go without saying that the vast majority of people are not as good at achieving the relevant push and pull as creative geniuses like Einstein and Picasso. Doing so is a difficult task. And that's not where the difficulty ends, for even once someone has achieved an appropriate balance, it's by no means a fait accompli that their imaginings will lead to creative results. But for those of us who don't have the imaginative capabilities of creative geniuses, must we simply accept this fact as our lot in life, or is there anything we can do to improve our situation? When it comes to creativity, philosophers have long disagreed about how to answer this question. We'll turn to this and related issues in Section 4.2.

4.2 Imagination and Creativity as Skills

The debate about whether creativity can be taught goes back to antiquity. On one side of the debate we find those who see creativity as an innate capacity, one that is sometimes described in divine terms as a gift of the Gods. Defenders of this view include writers such as Shakespeare and Coleridge as well as philosophers such as Plato and Kant; more recently a similar view has been defended by Peter Kivy (2001). As depicted in Plato's dialogues, Socrates often describes poetic creation as the result of divine inspiration; in the *Phaedrus*, for example, he characterizes such poets as becoming possessed by the Muses and experiencing a frenzied madness that awakens their lyrical powers. He offers a similar picture in the *Ion*, "a poet is a light and winged thing, and holy, and never able to compose until he has become inspired, and is beside himself, and reason is no longer in him" (Plato 1961, 220). On the other side of the debate we find philosophers who see creativity as a virtue that can be inculcated or a skill that can be developed. There are hints of this view in Aristotle, who in contrast to Plato saw poetic creation as a rational activity.[33] But we see a fuller development of the claim in recent works by philosophers such as Robert Audi (2018), who offers ways that creativity can be nurtured by educators, and Alan Hájek (2018) who offers heuristics one can use in an effort to spur creativity. I come down on Audi and Hájek's side of the debate. To my mind, creativity is best thought of as a skill that can be taught, as can other skills. More on this in a moment.

If creativity is a skill, and imagination typically undergirds it, then one might naturally expect that imagination would be a skill as well. And indeed, there are various places throughout the imagination literature where one encounters claims of this sort. To give just one example, Paul Taylor notes that exercising imagination is "to engage a particular mental skill" (1981, 206). There are also places where one encounters the claim that imaginative capacities vary from

---

[33] As described by Gaut, on the Aristotelian view "poetic creation is a rational activity of making, involving the selection and refinement of suitable goals and the use of the best means to achieve them" (Gaut 2012).

person to person or that imaginative tasks vary in difficulty from one to another. Alan White, for example, claims without elaboration that "To imagine that p . . . requires the exercise of a power, which some people may possess in greater degree than others" (1990, 138). Relatedly, Jennifer Gosetti-Ferencei has recently suggested that, though imagining is "remarkably easy" at times, different imaginative tasks will require more or less effort and "the degree of effort will vary according to the degree and complexity [of the task] and the facilities of the imaginer" (2018, 86).

In recent work, I have built upon these suggestions and put forth a skills-based framework for imagination (Kind 2020). Though there is not a philosophical consensus on what exactly skill is, there does seem to be some general agreement about some of the features that are typical of skilled activities.[34] My framework focuses on three such features:

1. First, when an activity is a skill, that activity is something that can be done more or less well. How exactly a performance is judged as better or worse will depend on the activity in question, but factors that might be relevant include such things as speed (as in sprinting or puzzle solving), distance (as in the long jump or javelin throwing), quantity (as in weight lifting), accuracy (as in archery), grace (as in ballroom dancing), beauty (as in art), evocativeness (as in poetry, art, and literature) and originality (also as in poetry, art, and literature).

2. Second, skilled activities are under the intentional control of the person engaged in the activity. As Gilbert Ryle notes, a skilled clown "trips and tumbles just as clumsy people do, except that he trips and tumbles on purpose and after much rehearsal and at the golden moment and where the children can see him and so as not to hurt himself" (1949, 33). Unlike the clumsy person's stumbles, the clown's stumbles are deliberate and controlled, and that's a large part of what makes the clown skilled at what he does.

3. Third, skills can be improved via practice or training. This practice may involve working with a trainer, observation of others, or solo efforts – or some combination of all three. In whatever manner the practice proceeds, however, repetitive efforts will be involved.

All three of these features apply to imagination. Our earlier discussion of imagination has already revealed ways that imagination embodies the first two of these features. In both its instructive and its transcendent uses, we've seen various examples of how imagination might be done more or less well.

---

[34] See Fridland and Pavese 2020 for a useful resource on skill.

Here the relevant factors typically won't involve speed or distance. For instructive purposes, accuracy will likely be important, whereas for transcendent purposes, factors such as beauty and originality may come into play, along with various other aesthetic considerations. As for the feature of intentional control, we've seen that imagining is a voluntary activity that is subject to the will.

But what about the third feature? How might imagination be improved via practice or training? Though it's relatively easy to think of ways that one might train to become a better ballroom dancer, or javelin thrower, or puzzle solver, how might one train to become a better imaginer?

Interestingly, this topic has not been the subject of much discussion in either the philosophical literature or the empirical literature (though see Kind 2022). Psychologists and other researchers working on imagination do often treat it as a skill. For example, Jennifer Cumming and Sarah Williams note that imagination is "a collection of skills that are modifiable with training and experience rather than simply a general, undifferentiated fixed ability" (2012, 222).[35] In their view, though some individuals are naturally disposed to find imagining easier than others, the subskills underlying imagining can be significantly honed to enable individuals to become proficient at imagining, even individuals who are not naturally disposed to find imagining easy. Having made these points, however, they also note that there has been surprisingly little attention paid to the question of how exactly one can do this, that is, the question of how an individual can effectively develop their imaginative skills.

One place we do see discussion of this issue in the philosophical literature comes in the treatment of empathy (or what we can think of as *empathetic imagination*) and, in particular, in the work of Martha Nussbaum. We have earlier touched on this kind of imagination via our vignette, Empathetic Explorations. As we saw, empathetic imagination is a kind of experiential imagination. On Nussbaum's view, literature and other forms of storytelling play a critical role in the cultivation of our capacity for this type of imagination, for these kinds of works have "the power to make us see the lives of the different with more than a casual tourist's interest – with involvement and sympathetic understanding" (1997, 88). This process begins in childhood, where a child who engages with stories starts to develop a capacity for attributing thoughts and

---

[35] Cumming and Williams talk of "imagery" rather than "imagination" and, in fact, psychologists and other empirical researchers tend to favor talk of mental imagery as opposed to imagination as a matter of general practice. It seems clear, however, that what they mean by imagery is akin to what philosophers mean by imagination, at least when it comes to imagistic or experiential imagination.

emotions to animals and to other humans and thereby also develops a capacity for coming to understand them. Without these stories, says Nussbaum, this imaginative development would not be possible:

> A child deprived of stories is deprived, as well, of certain ways of viewing other people. For the insides of people, like the insides of stars, are not open to view. They must be wondered about. And the conclusion that this set of limbs in front of me has emotions and feelings and thoughts of the sort I attribute to myself will not be reached without the training of the imagination that storytelling promotes. (1997, 89)

This kind of training continues throughout life via an individual's encounters with increasingly sophisticated works of literature. When engaging with the text, the reader gets opportunities to imaginatively put themselves in the characters' shoes, and to imaginatively explore what those characters are feeling. In introducing readers to a diversity of characters facing a diversity of situations, including many that the reader will not themselves have experienced, stories allow the reader to practice empathizing – and moreover, they can do so in a safe context where the stakes are relatively low.

Echoes of Nussbaum's point can often be found in writers' own reflections on their work. Science fiction author Ursula Le Guin notes that "one of the best exercises for the imagination, maybe the very best, is hearing, reading, and telling or writing made-up stories" (Le Guin 2016, 109). Importantly, the point can be extended beyond literature and storytelling to other forms of art. For example, George Eliot has noted that:

> The greatest benefit we owe to the artist, whether painter, poet, or novelist, is the extension of our sympathies. Appeals founded on generalizations and statistics required a sympathy ready-made, a moral sentiment already in activity; but a picture of human life such as a great artist can give, surprises even the trivial and the selfish into that attention to what is apart from themselves, which may be called the raw material of moral sentiment. . . . Art is the nearest thing to life; it is a mode of amplifying experience and extending our contact with our fellow-men beyond the bounds of our personal lot. (1990, 110)

As this discussion suggests, engagement with storytelling can be a training ground for the empathetic imagination. But it soon becomes clear that storytelling can provide a training ground for other kinds of imagination as well. We not only imagine how characters feel but we imagine how they look. We also imagine the surroundings they occupy and the places that they go. We imaginatively anticipate what might happen next, and we imaginatively explore different possible endings the story might have.

Imagination might also be practiced by engaging in the kinds of imagination-stretching techniques found in the kinds of games and warmups used in classes and workshops on improv comedy. These kinds of activities help one to break out of a set mentality, to improve receptivity to new ideas, and to think quickly on one's feet. In many ways, they are reminiscent of the kinds of activities often used to measure creativity. In the Incomplete Figure Test, subjects are given a picture (often it is just a squiggly line of some sort) and asked to incorporate it into a picture and to give the picture a title. In the Alternative Uses test, subjects are asked to come up with as many alternative uses as they can in a set time period for a specified common object (like a brick or a paper clip). The test score is determined by not only how many uses the subject comes up with but also the number of different categories those uses fall into and how uncommon the answers are.

These "thinking outside the box" kinds of training activities seem especially helpful for transcendent imagination and the removal of constraints, but we can also think of activities that would be more helpful for instructive imagination and the imposition of constraints. In my own work, I've suggested one might use what we might think of as imaginative matching activities. Pairing up with a friend (or "trainer"), an individual might try to match their imaginings to descriptions given. I envision this happening via the use of a children's picture book of dinosaurs or sea creatures or construction vehicles. The trainer describes one of the pictured dinosaurs (or sea creatures or construction vehicles) in as much detail as they can. The imaginer then tries to imagine the object described. Once they think they have done it, they are shown the picture and they can evaluate how well they did. Though they won't be able to get direct corrective feedback from the trainer, since the trainer doesn't have access to the imagining produced, the individual can make judgments for themselves about how close their imagining matched the object described. Of course, the usefulness of this exercise depends, at least in part, on the quality of the descriptions that the trainer produces. But this is no different from any kind of training since, as a general matter, the quality of training exercises rests on the quality of the trainer.

If imagination undergirds creativity, and imagination can be trained, then that gives us reason to think that creativity can be trained as well. The kinds of imagination-stretching exercises just discussed seem perfectly suited toward enabling novelty, and depending on how they are structured, they could be well suited for achieving value as well (see also the techniques discussed by Hájek (2018)). Contra Plato, we do not need to await inspiration from the muses to develop our imaginative and creative capacities. Rather, the power to do so lies with us.

5 A Case Study: Imagination and Creativity in Machines

Having begun to flesh out our understanding of the relationship between imagination and creativity by way of the discussion of Section 4, I turn now to a case study that will help us to explore these issues in more detail. Explosive developments in computing and AI over the last several decades have led to machines that demonstrate a multitude of different capacities. In 2011, IBM's Watson famously came out on top in a *Jeopardy!* match against two of the world's best players, while DeepMind's AlphaGo became the first computer program to defeat a world champion Go player in 2016. We now regularly rely on computer personal assistant programs such as Siri and Alexa to manage all sorts of tasks for us. And there are already self-driving cars on the roads around us. While all of these advances contribute to a growing optimism about the possibility of thinking machines, there are other advances that contribute to a growing optimism about the possibility of creative machines. In particular, there exist machines that compose music (like David Cope's experiments in musical intelligence (EMI)), write poetry (like Ray Kurzweil's Cybernetic Poet or Zackary Scholl's poetry generator), generate jokes and other forms of humor (like Kim Binsted's JAPE), and – as we will discuss in more detail in Sections 5.1 and 5.2 – paint and draw. Recent years have witnessed machine-generated works of art and music that are so increasingly sophisticated that they are practically indiscernible from works produced by humans, so much so that one might think that creative machines are not just a possibility but an actuality. Consider *The Portrait of Edmond de Belamy*, a 70 × 70 cm Inkjet portrait created by an AI program. In 2018, this portrait sold for the astounding sum of $432,500 at an auction at Christie's. To put this sale price in context, note that at the same auction, an Andy Warhol print sold for $75,000, while a piece by Roy Lichtenstein sold for $87,500.

In this section, we will look more closely at machine "artists" and the artworks they generate in an effort to explore whether and to what extent machines can engage in imagination and be creative. Though the Christie's sale might suggest that these questions have already been settled in the affirmative, matters are not quite so simple, and many (perhaps even most) of the issues about machine creativity and machine imagination are in need of significant philosophical attention. By exploring these issues in this section, not only will we be in a better position to judge whether creativity and imagination should be attributed to machines, but we will also be helped to better understand these two individual phenomena themselves and the relationship between them.

5.1 Aaron

In the 1960s, British painter Harold Cohen was in the midst of a thriving career in art. He was a member of the Visual Arts Department at the Slade School of Fine Arts in London and was regularly putting on exhibitions of his work in both galleries and museums. In the early 1970s, however, Cohen began a study of AI. Bringing his two different interests in contact with one another, Cohen set to work writing a computer program with the aim of creating a machine that would exhibit cognitive capabilities similar to the ones that humans use when drawing and interpreting images (Cohen 1995). The result was a system he called Aaron. While early versions of Aaron were fairly unsophisticated in their capabilities, enabling the machine to distinguish closed figures from open figures and perform very simple manipulations of those figures, later versions became increasingly more capable. By 1985, Aaron had been programmed with a set of rules about the world that enabled it to produce images such as "Liberty and Friends," a drawing that depicts a colorful series of Statue of Liberty figures. In subsequent development of the program, Cohen provided it with a voluminous set of rules governing three-dimensionality, bodily structures, physical features and facial types, and haircuts. To get a sense of the enormity of this set of rules, note that 4,000 of them were devoted solely to how to draw a head! With all these rules in place, the drawings produced by the machine (by way of a robotic arm) began to look more interesting and more realistic. By 1995, newspapers like the *Washington Post* were running stories on Aaron with headlines such as: "Is Aaron's work creative art or just high-tech doodling?" The answer, at least according to one museum director quoted in the piece, is that a machine like Aaron "debunks" the idea that creativity should be viewed as exclusively human.

Cohen himself has also addressed this question. In a video clip from the 1987 film *The Age of Intelligent Machines*, inventor and futurist Raymond Kurzweil asked Cohen about the possibility of machine creativity:

> Kurzweil: Is the computer being creative?
> Cohen: I think creativity is a relative term. Clearly the machine is being creative, the program is being creative, to the degree that every time it does a drawing it does a drawing that nobody has ever seen before, including me. I don't think it's currently as creative as I am in writing the program. I think for a program to be fully creative, in a more complete sense creative, it has to be able to modify its own performance, and that's a very difficult problem.

Cohen here seems perfectly content to judge Aaron's outputs to be creative, that is, to accept that the machine achieves product-creativity. This assessment aligns well with a conception of product-creativity in terms of novelty and value. Clearly, the drawings are novel, and they would seem to satisfy the value requirement as well – at least given the deflationary sense of value that we've been working with. It's when we turn to the additional requirements that are often included in definitions of creativity – the surprisingness and the agency requirements – that the judgment of Aaron's drawings as creative seems more questionable.

It's easier to see the issues raised by these two requirements if we shift our focus from product-creativity to process-creativity. The rules with which Aaron has been programmed enable it to continue indefinitely its production of new paintings in accordance with those rules. Moreover, over the years Cohen has given Aaron an increasing number of rules. But Aaron does not have the capability to transcend those rules. It cannot adapt or modify the rules that it has been given or learn new rules on its own. The only way for it to gain additional capabilities is via additional programming by Cohen. As a result, it's not clear that the processes used by Aaron could evince the kind of surprisingness that a thinker like Boden demands. Certainly, these processes will not achieve transformational creativity, the kind of creativity that involves transforming an existing space, and it looks unlikely that they could even achieve exploratory creativity. At best, insofar as these processes involve Aaron in putting together new combinations of shapes and colors in the course of its drawings, there might be a kind of combinatorial creativity involved.

It seems even less likely that the processes Aaron uses could meet the agency requirement for creativity than that they could meet the surprisingness requirement. First, it seems implausible that Aaron counts as an intentional agent. But even if it did, that wouldn't necessarily mean that the processes used in the production of his paintings would meet the agency requirement; as we saw in our earlier discussion of that requirement, not every action by an intentional agent will count as an exercise of intentional agency. Some are simply accidental. Moreover, recall Gaut's example of a painter who creates a work of art by way of a paint-by-numbers technique. The painter's actions in this case are intentional. But, as Gaut suggested, since the painter is simply following a set of specified rules and is not exercising any individual judgment, it doesn't look like the processes utilized satisfy the agency requirement. If this is right, then there's no question that Aaron's processes wouldn't satisfy it either. Aaron's drawings are produced entirely by following a set of specified rules, and it doesn't even have any mechanisms for exercising individual judgment. Perhaps it's these kinds of considerations that Cohen has in mind when he denies that Aaron can be "fully" creative or creative "in a more complete sense."

Similar points apply to many of the other systems often touted as creative machines. Consider, for example, David Cope's composing machine, EMI. EMI has been programmed to compose new music in the style of a particular classical composer that it has studied. In describing EMI's compositional processes, Cope notes that they involve the deconstruction of material into separately analyzable parts, identification of that material's musical signatures, and then a recombination of the identified parts into new works while retaining the identified musical signature.

The various AI poetry generators that have been developed operate using roughly similar principles. Consider Ray Kurzweil's Cybernetic Poet (RKCP). The program is provided with a sample of a given poet's work and then creates a model of the poet's style based on words, word and rhythm patterns, and the overall poetic structure. Algorithms enable RKCP to select what word to use at which point, to end a particular line of poetry, to end the poem as a whole, and so on, and thereby enable RKCP to produce complete poems. In Kurzweil's view, though "the poems have a similar style to the author(s) originally analyzed," they are nonetheless "completely original new poetry" (Kurzweil 2000).

Zackary Scholl's poetry generator uses a similar kind of algorithm to that used by RKCP. After first dissecting a poem into smaller components, the program randomly selects from among the elements in its database to sub in for each component, and it then "recursively generates each of those" (Scholl 2015). The poems produced were sufficiently indistinguishable from human-produced poems that one was even accepted for publication in an undergraduate literary magazine published by Duke University. As this strongly suggests, the computer-generated poem struck the magazine's editors as original and valu-able (assuming, that is, that publishability requires some measure of novelty and value – perhaps a questionable assumption!).

Just as was the case with Aaron, however, though these other systems may be able to meet the requirements of novelty and value, their rule-governed, recom-binatorial, and recursive approaches make it difficult to see them as meeting the requirement for surprisingness and even more difficult to see them as meeting the requirement for agency. They thus don't seem to provide us with compelling examples of computer creativity – or at least not computer creativity in any meaningful or deep sense.

It's even more difficult to see these machines as having employed any imagination in their artistic and poetic endeavors. Imagination is a species of mental activity. It is a species of thought. We can grant that it's in principle possible for machines to think. And we can even grant that the day is not too far off when there will exist such machines in practice. But the machines like Aaron and RKCP we have surveyed here do not appear to be thinking, and indeed they don't even come close. As such, they thus don't provide us with much insight into what machine imagination might be like. We'll thus postpone discussion of machine imagination until after we have another example before us.

5.2 Generative Adversarial Networks

At this point, one might reasonably wonder whether the problem is simply that we've been considering outdated examples. Perhaps a more compelling case for the creativity of machines might be provided by consideration of more contemporary examples. After all, Aaron's programming was initially developed more than forty years ago, and all of the examples thus far considered use traditional models of computing that might seem especially ill-suited to achieving true creativity. But what about the machine-produced Belamy portrait that sold for over $400,000 at Christie's just a few years ago? In this section, we'll consider whether the more innovative computer approach that led to the creation of that portrait might offer a better candidate for imagination and creativity in machines.

The Obvious Collective, the human group behind the Belamy portrait, produces their computer-generated artworks via a technique known as generative adversarial networks (or GANs). GANs entered the scene via work in 2014 by PhD student Ian Goodfellow. To understand Goodfellow's innovative work, we need to put it in the context of connectionism, a kind of computing that was first conceived of in the 1940s but then exploded in the 1980s. Connectionist networks operate differently from traditionally programmed computers in that they use parallel processing, with many different interconnected information-processing units working simultaneously. The connections between units are not all the same but have different strengths that are adjusted by way of a training process that enables the computer to produce the outputs desired by the programmers. Drawing upon the basic connectionist architectures already in use, Goodfellow's innovation was to put two different networks in competition with one another.

In a GAN, the two adversarial networks are both initially trained on a set of exemplars of a certain type. For example, they might be given pictures of dogs or sofas or human faces. One network, the generator, is then given the task of generating an image that depicts a new example of the same type. The second network, the discriminator, is given the task of determining whether an image presented to it is a genuine exemplar of the type or one of the facsimiles produced by the generator. The generator "wins" if it produces facsimiles that fool the discriminator; the discriminator "wins" if it is able to successfully sort the real examples from the fake examples. As the networks compete against each other, the competition provides them each with feedback on how they're doing, and they make adjustments accordingly. The generator adjusts the various parameters it uses in creating new examples, and it thus starts producing examples that are more and more realistic. The discriminator adjusts the various parameters it uses in differentiating the examples, so it gets better at telling the real from the fake. But at a certain point, the generator gets so good at its task that the images it produces are impressively realistic – so much so, that they will fool not only the discriminator network but also humans.

Though they describe themselves as "driven by a fascination for replicating creativity," the Obvious Collective is hesitant to herald their GANs as creative machines. This hesitancy stems largely from the prominent role played by humans in the process of creating art via algorithms. Not only do humans develop the algorithms that lead to the artwork's production, but they also choose the subject of the artwork, curate the training data that will be provided to the GANs, select which output from the GANs to use, and select the medium by which the art will be displayed. For example, in the Belamy case, the humans wrote the algorithm used, decided the relevant kind of artwork would be portraiture, put together the training dataset containing more than 15,000 portraits produced over the past 700 years, and decided that the Belamy portrait would be printed on canvas and then presented in a golden wooden frame. Going forward, however, the Obvious Collective expects that human involvement in the overall process will gradually diminish until at some point the whole process is done by the machine. Once that happens, they would no longer be cautious in their descriptions: "Once the whole process will have been automated, we will have created a machine that is capable of being creative, in the same way a human is" (Obvious 2020).

Many of the news stories and commentaries describing the Belamy portrait were also cautious, with a number of writers not only disparaging the work's artistic merits but also rejecting any claims about the creativity of the process that produced it. In an article in the *Smithsonian* magazine, digital art blogger Jason Bailey suggests that it's well recognized that the algorithms currently in play in AI art are "not active collaborators or autonomous agents" (Solly 2018). That said, some commentators were considerably less cautious. To give just one example, the headline of an article in *Technology Review* describes Goodfellow, the inventor of GANs, as "The man who's given machines the gift of imagination" (Giles 2018). When looking more closely at the article's claims, however, it becomes clear that the rhetoric of the headline was somewhat overblown – even by the article's own standards. In the article itself, the goal is described more modestly not as providing the machines with imagination but as providing them with "something akin to imagination." Moreover, the article notes that the machine's imagination-like power is still limited. Though it predicts that in the future computers will "get much better at feasting on raw data and working out what they need to learn from it without being told," it doesn't explain how this would amount to an increase in the machines' imaginative capabilities.

Ultimately, then, it looks like the GANs producing artwork do not fare much better than older machines like Aaron when it comes to creativity and imagination. As was the case with Aaron's artworks, the artworks produced by the GANs might meet novelty and value requirements for product-creativity. But they falter with respect to both the surprisingness and the agency requirements, and the processes involved again seem to work by a kind of blind algorithm rather than by way of imagination. Granted, the GANs processing is quite unlike Aaron's processing. Unlike Aaron, GANs don't work in terms of blind rule-following. There are no rules programmed into the system to tell the GANs whether one image is more or less like a given exemplar than another.[36] Although human learning and creativity often involves trial and error, the trial-and-error processes used by the GANs seem to work more by brute force than by the guided cognitive manipulation we associate with creativity. Though the analogy isn't a perfect one, the GANs seem akin to Charles Goodyear, who happened upon a way of vulcanizing rubber by way of a lucky accident. If you mix rubber with enough different kinds of substances, at some point you'll probably find one that works. Your process might not be entirely accidental. What you learn from some of your initial efforts might inform your subsequent ones. But it's still hard to see the procedure as a creative one. There's not really any imagination involved. Likewise, if you produce enough new images based on some exemplars that you've been shown, at some point you'll probably find one that works. Yes, you'll have achieved success. Unfortunately, however, the achievement of success is not the same as the achievement of creative success.

5.3 A Remaining Question

Of course, even if no existing machines are appropriately described as creative or as engaging in imagination, this doesn't mean that machine creativity and imagination are in principle impossible. But that raises an obvious question: How will we be able to tell when machines have reached that milestone?

The problem is especially pressing in light of our example of the Portrait of Edmond de Belamy. Though not all critics agreed that it actually had artistic value, many did. Moreover, a proponent of machine creativity might accuse the

---

[36] See Langland-Hassan 2020, 286–288 for discussion of how the processing utilized by GANs is different from rule-following. Langland-Hassan's conclusions about the implications it has for creativity of GANs are more optimistic than mine.

negative critics of a kind of human-centric bias. If the portrait had been produced by a human creator rather than by a machine, they might say, there would be no question about its artistic value. Even if is not quite true about this particular portrait, it's fairly easy to imagine that the next generation of GANs will be capable of producing an artwork about which this could be said. So if we wouldn't withhold a judgment of creativity from the human-produced art, why withhold it from the machine-produced art? Shouldn't we be careful not to hold the machines to an unreasonably high standard, one that is much higher than the one to which we hold one another? Perhaps what it means for a machine to be creative is very different from what it means for a human to be creative (for useful discussion, see Halina 2021).

Though I am focusing here on creativity in machines, it's worth noting at least briefly that similar issues might be raised about animal creativity (see, e.g., Mitchell 2016). Consider Ruby, an Asian elephant who lived most of her life in the Phoenix Zoo. After seeing her scratching in the dirt with a stick, a zoo employee decided to provide her with painting equipment. Holding the paintbrush with her trunk, Ruby created paintings that art critics compare to the kind of abstract artworks created by Willem de Kooning and Jackson Pollock (Higgins 2020). Just as we might ask whether Aaron the machine exhibited creativity in its paintings, we might also ask whether Ruby the elephant exhibited creativity in her painting.

At the start of our discussion of machine creativity and imagination, I made an analogy to machine thought. In considering these kinds of worries, we can now see the aptness of that analogy, as much the same kind of dialectic plays out in that context that we now see playing out in this one. Consider the famous Turing Test developed by Alan Turing in 1950. According to Turing, if a machine can produce intelligent output that is sufficiently like the output of a human, so much so that a neutral interrogator could not tell the difference, then we should judge the computer to be thinking. In Turing's view, the question "Can machines think?," asked that way, is "too meaningless to deserve discussion" (Turing 1950). It invites too much controversy about what the word "thinking" means, and it is too easy to produce definitions of thinking that beg the question against those who want to apply this attribute to machines. Perhaps, then, the proponent of machine creativity should take a similar line: Instead of trying to define creativity and then seeing whether that definition could be applied to a machine's processes, we should bypass the issue altogether and simply declare that if a machine can produce creative output that would fool a neutral interrogator, we should judge the computer to be creative. This line of response has recently been articulated by Melvin Chen:

> To ask for a rigorous definition of [the] mental state of creativity and the
> creative uses of the imagination is to miss the entire point . . . . We do not need
> a definition of creativity or the creative uses of the imagination to see that
> once we can no longer tell machine-produced creative output apart from
> human-produced creative output, we will not have a basis for denying of
> one (viz. the imagination machine) what we typically affirm of the other (viz.
> creative human individuals). (2018, 284)

In fact, as Chen notes, some explorations of machine creativity are already
proceeding in precisely this vein. From 2016 to 2018, the Neukomb Institute for
Computational Science ran an annual competition that they called the *Creative
Turing Test*. The challenges offered ranged across various creative domains
including poetry, short stories, jazz composition, choreography, and the production of dance music DJ sets. In these competitions, the machines were usually
easily distinguishable from humans.[37]

Of course, the Creative Turing Test is open to many of the same objections as
the Turing Test. Some of these objections were considered by Turing in his
original discussion of the test. One that might seem especially relevant to the
Creative Turing Test is what Turing called *Lady Lovelace's Objection*. Talking
specifically about the Analytical Engine, a hypothetical machine proposed by
Charles Babbage in 1837, Lady Lovelace noted that such a computer "has no
pretensions to *originate anything*. It can do *whatever we know how to order it* to
perform" (as quoted in Turing (1950)). In his discussion of this objection,
Turing notes that we might interpret it (or a close variant of it) as charging
that a machine can never really do anything new or that a machine can never
take us by surprise. As such, there are some obvious responses that can be made
by the proponent of creative machines.

First, in line with the distinction between P-creativity and H-creativity,
someone might note that genuine newness is not required for P-creativity.
Second, they might note that programmers often cannot come close to predict-
ing exactly what outputs will be produced by their own programs, and they are
often surprised by what their programs produce. On Turing's view, the main
reason we are tempted to think that machines cannot surprise us is the fallacious
assumption that "as soon as a fact is presented to a mind all consequences of that
fact spring into the mind simultaneously with it" (Turing 1950). A related way to
respond to this objection is offered by Chen, who notes that in a machine-
learning context, as we have with GANs, "algorithms have the capacity to
define or modify their decision-making rules autonomously" (Chen 2018,
286). Since these modifications cannot be predicted in advance by the human

---

[37] You can explore this for yourself with respect to the dance music DJ sets by checking out the
competitors in an online poll available at http://bregman.dartmouth.edu/turingtests/DJPoll

programmers, the outputs of their machines could surprise them even if they were able to extrapolate all the consequences of their original program.

So, it looks like Lady Lovelace's objection can probably be set to rest. But there is another objection that cannot be so easily handled. Turing considers it under the guise of the *Argument from Consciousness*. In brief, the worry is that it's not enough for a machine to produce some output; rather, the machine also has to be conscious of the output that it produced. When it comes to thinking, Turing tries to hold the objection at bay by way of a kind of argument known as *reductio ad absurdum*, that is, by showing that it leads to an absurd conclusion: "the only way by which one could be sure that a machine thinks is to *be* the machine and to feel oneself thinking. Likewise according to this view the only way to know that a *man* thinks is to be that particular man" (Turing 1950). Turing thinks that one would be better off abandoning the argument from consciousness than being forced to embrace solipsism.

With respect to creativity, however, we might think that the argument from consciousness has particular bite. The problem is not that creativity must always arise fully consciously. There are many examples from history where a creative idea just came to someone "in a flash," or where the idea just hits them upon waking up from a good night's sleep. In such cases, they may have no idea what kinds of cognitive processes they used that led to the idea. But despite these kinds of cases, our earlier discussion has shown us that the kind of cognitive process underlying creativity does matter. In short, the problem is that not just any old cognitive process will do. As we have discussed, procedures involving blind rule-following, mere brute force, and so on, are not sufficient for process-creativity, and insofar as process-creativity is often important for product-creativity and person-creativity, these procedures will not be sufficient for those kinds of creativity either. As someone tempted by the agency requirement might say, the problem is that the computer lacks agency over anything that it does.

Insofar as the determination of whether a machine can be creative involves a focus on the underlying process of the machine, it suggests that we're looking for the machine to be doing something like imagining in order to be comfortable attributing creativity to it. As we noted earlier in Section 4.1.1 when raising worries for the necessity claim, imagination might not be strictly necessary for creativity. But as we also noted, imagination and creativity nonetheless seem very tightly connected, with imagination taken to be the primary means of achieving creativity even though there might be other such means as well. Practically speaking, then, the question of whether a machine can be creative can be seen to reduce to the question of whether a machine can have imagination. We should once again be careful about human-centric bias. It might be that machine creativity involves different kinds of processes from human creativity. But thinking about the needed process along the lines of imagination helps us to see why the Creative Turing Tests strike us as falling short.

We noted earlier that Turing thought that pushing too hard on worries about machine consciousness would lead to solipsism. Does the line of argumentation about machine imagination just considered force us to an analogous position, a view on which one cannot know that any creature other than oneself engages in imagination? I'm inclined to think that we can resist this problematic result. The way we know that other humans have exercised their imagination is not just by looking at their creative outputs but by talking to them about their creative processes. It's their descriptions of their mental activities that incline us to see them as imagining. Thus, perhaps an assessment of machine creativity will have to await the day when machines develop not only the capacities for creative output but also the capacities to explain to us how they got to that output. Let's be careful about what exactly this claim amounts to. The claim is not that the ability to provide such explanations is itself a requirement for creativity. Perhaps a being – human or machine – can be creative without being able to offer any reflections on their cognitive processes. But in order for us to make judgments about creativity, such explanations may end up playing a crucial role.

6 Conclusion

Philosophical work on imagination and creativity has blossomed in recent years, and it is an exciting time to be thinking about these issues. Over the course of this Element, we have explored both imagination and creativity, and we have also explored the connection between them. As we have seen, though imagination is neither necessary nor sufficient for creativity, these two activities do frequently or even typically go together. While there are other means of achieving creativity, imagination is a primary (or perhaps even *the* primary) means to this end.

One important theme throughout my discussion concerns the fact that imagination and creativity should not be seen as fixed, immutable capacities but rather as skills that can be improved. Given the importance that imagination and creativity play in a large multitude of contexts, we would all do well to work to improve our own imaginative and creative abilities. Though this Element was not meant to be a How-To Guide in this regard, as was acknowledged at the start, the discussion has revealed some ways that we might start going about this.

Our understanding of imagination and creativity develops primarily from thinking about human imagination and human creativity. As became clear in the final section of this Element, however, there are numerous examples of machines that produce outputs we might naturally describe as imaginative or creative, and it seems clear that the future will bring even more impressive machine achievements. Going forward, it seems reasonable to expect that such achievements will pose new challenges to philosophical thinking about imagination and creativity, and there will likely be increasing pressure to expand our understanding of these capabilities beyond the human context. Personally, I look forward to seeing how this future philosophical work develops, and I hope that this Element has succeeded not only in surveying the current terrain in philosophy of imagination and philosophy of creativity but also in laying the foundation needed for the continuation of these explorations in years to come.

References

Almeida, Dennis F., and George G. Joseph. 2004. "Eurocentrism in the History of Mathematics: The Case of the Kerala School." *Race and Class* 45 (4): 45–59.

Audi, Robert. 2018. "Creativity, Imagination, and Intellectual Virtue." In *Creativity and Philosophy*, edited by Berys Gaut and Matthew Kieran, 25–41. Abingdon: Routledge.

Balcerak Jackson, Magdalena. 2016. "On the Epistemic Value of Imagining, Supposing, and Conceiving." In *Knowledge through Imagination*, edited by Amy Kind and Peter Kung, 41–60. Oxford: Oxford University Press.

Boden, Margaret. 1990/2005. *The Creative Mind: Myths and Mechanisms*. 2nd ed. Abingdon: Routledge.

Boden, Margaret. 1994. *Dimensions of Creativity*. Cambridge, MA: The MIT Press.

Bradley, Ryan. 2014. "A Brief History of Failure." *The New York Times*, November 12. www.nytimes.com/interactive/2014/11/12/magazine/16inno vationsfailures.html

Brann, Eva. 1991. *The World of Imagination*. Lanham, MD: Rowman and Littlefield.

Brown, James Robert, and Yiftach Fehige. 2019. "Thought Experiment." *Stanford Encyclopedia of Philosophy*. Edited by Edward N. Zalta. https:// plato.stanford.edu/entries/thought-experiment/

Campbell, John W. 1966. "Introduction." In *Analog 6*, edited by John W. Campbell, ix–xvi. Garden City, NY: Doubleday.

Chen, Melvin. 2018. "Imagination Machines, Dartmouth-based Turing Tests, & a Potted History of Responses." *AI & Society* 35: 283–287.

Cohen, Harold. 1995. "The Further Exploits of Aaron, Painter." *Stanford Humanities Review* 4 (2): 141–158.

Cumming, Jennifer, and Sarah E. Williams. 2012. "The Role of Imagery in Performance." In *The Oxford Handbook of Sport and Performance Psychology*, edited by Shane E. Murphy, 231–232. Oxford: Oxford University Press. http://doi.org/10.1093/oxfordhb/9780199731763.013.0011

Currie, Gregory. 2002. "Desire in Imagination." In *Conceivability and Possibility*, edited by Tamar Gendler and John Hawthorne, 201–221. Oxford: Oxford University Press.

Currie, Gregory, and Ian Ravenscroft. 2002. *Recreative Minds*. Oxford: Oxford University Press.

Doggett, Tyler, and Andy Egan. 2007. "Wanting Things You Don't Want." *Philosophers' Imprint* 7: 1–17.

Dorsch, Fabian. 2012. *The Unity of Imagining*. Berlin: De Gruyter. http://doi.org/10.1515/9783110325966

Eliot, George. 1990. *Selected Essays, Poems, and Other Writings*. Edited by Antonia. S. Byatt and Nicholas Warren. London: Penguin Books.

Feynman, Richard. 1965/2017. *The Character of Physical Law*. Cambridge, MA: The MIT Press.

Fforde, Jasper. 2003. *The Well of Lost Plots*. New York: Penguin Books.

Fridland, Ellen, and Carlotta Pavese. 2020. *Routledge Handbook on Skill and Expertise*. Abingdon: Routledge.

Galton, Francis. 1880. "Statistics of Mental Imagery." *Mind* 5: 301–318.

Gaut, Berys. 2012. "Creativity and Rationality." *The Journal of Aesthetics and Art Criticism* 70 (3): 259–270.

Gaut, Berys. 2010. "The Philosophy of Creativity." *Philosophy Compass* 5 (12): 1034–1046.

Gaut, Berys. 2018. "The Value of Creativity." In *Creativity and Philosophy*, edited by Berys Gaut and Matthew Kieran, 124–139. Abingdon: Routledge.

Gaut, Berys, and Matthew Kieran. 2018. "Philosophising about Creativity." In *Creativity and Philosophy*, edited by Berys Gaut and Matthew Kieran, 1–21. Abingdon: Routledge.

Gendler, Tamar. 2003. "On the Relation between Pretense and Belief." In *Imagination, Philosophy, and the Arts*, edited by Matthew Kieran and Dominic McIver Lopes, 125–141. Abingdon: Routledge.

Gendler, Tamar. 2000. "The Puzzle of Imaginative Resistance." *Journal of Philosophy* 97 (2): 55–81.

Giles, Martin. 2018. "The GANfather: The Man Who's Given Machines the Gift of Imagination." *Technology Review*, February 21. www.technologyreview.com/2018/02/21/145289/the-ganfather-the-man-whos-given-machines-the-gift-of-imagination/

Gosetti-Ferencei, Jennifer. 2018. *The Life of Imagination: Revealing and Making the World*. New York: Columbia University Press.

Gottlieb, Rebecca J. M., Elizabeth Hyde, Mary Helen Immordino-Yang, and Scott Barry Kaufman. 2019. "Imagination is the Seed of Creativity." In *The Cambridge Handbook of Creativity*, edited by James C. Kaufman and Robert J. Sternberg, 709–731. Cambridge: Cambridge University Press.

Grady, Denise. 2020. "Trial of Coronavirus Vaccine Made by Moderna Begins in Seattle." *The New York Times*, March 16. www.nytimes.com/2020/03/16/health/coronavirus-vaccine.html

Grant, James. 2018. "Creativity as an Artistic Merit." In *Creativity and Philosophy*, edited by Berys Gaut and Matthew Kieran, 333–349. Abingdon: Routledge.

Hájek, Alan. 2018. "Creating Heuristics for Philosophical Creativity." In *Creativity and Philosophy*, edited by Berys Gaut and Matthew Kieran, 292–312. Abingdon: Routledge.

Halina, Marta. 2021. "Insightful Artificial Intelligence." *Mind and Language* 36: 315–329.

Higgins, Grace. 2020. "Art Pieces Painted by Elephants Have Been Sold for Over $25,000." *InideTonight*, July 22. https://insidetonight.com/art-pieces-painted-by-elephants-have-been-sold-for-over-25000/

Hills, Alison, and Alexander Bird. 2018. "Creativity without Value." In *Creativity and Philosophy*, edited by Berys Gaut and Dustin Stokes, 95–107. Abingdon: Routledge.

Hounshell, David A. 1975. "Elisha Gray and the Telephone: On the Disadvantages of Being an Expert." *Technology and Culture* 16 (2): 133–161.

Hume, David. 1777/1977. *An Enquiry Concerning Human Understanding*. Edited by Eric Steinberg. Indianapolis, IN: Hackett.

Hume, David. 1739/1985. *A Treatise of Human Nature*. Edited by Peter. H. Nidditch. Oxford: Oxford University Press.

James, William. 1889. "The Psychology of Belief." *Mind* 14 (55): 321–352.

Kieran, Matthew. 2014. "Creativity, Virtue and the Challenges from Natural Talent, Ill-Being and Immorality." *Royal Institute of Philosophy Supplements* 75: 203–230.

Kind, Amy. 2018. "How Imagination Gives Rise to Knowledge." In *Perceptual Memory and Perceptual Presence*, edited by Fabian Dorsch and Fiona Macpherson, 227–246. Oxford: Oxford University Press.

Kind, Amy. 2017. "Imaginative Vividness." *Journal of the American Philosophical Association* 3: 32–50.

Kind, Amy. 2016. "Imagining under Constraints." In *Knowledge through Imagination*, edited by Amy Kind and Peter Kung, 145–159. Oxford: Oxford University Press.

Kind, Amy. 2022. "Learning to Imagine." *British Journal of Aesthetics* 62: 33–48. http://doi.org/10.1093/aesthj/ayab037

Kind, Amy. 2001. "Putting the Image Back in Imagination." *Philosophy and Phenomenological Research* 62: 85–109.

Kind, Amy. 2011. "The Puzzle of Imaginative Desire." *Australasian Journal of Philosophy* 89 (3): 421–439.

Kind, Amy. 2020. "The Skill of Imagination." In *The Routledge Handbook of Skill and Expertise*, edited by Ellen Fridland and Carlotta Pavese, 335–346. Abingdon: Routledge.

Kind, Amy, and Peter Kung. 2016. "Introduction: The Puzzle of Imaginative Use." In *Knowledge through Imagination*, edited by Amy Kind and Peter Kung, 1–37. Oxford: Oxford University Press.

Kivy, Peter. 2001. *The Possesor and the Possessed*. New Haven, CT: Yale University Press.

Kronfelder, Maria. 2009. "Creativity Naturalized." *The Philosophical Quarterly* 59 (237): 577–592.

Kung, Peter. 2010. "Imagining as a Guide to Possibility." *Philosophy and Phenomenological Research* 81 (3): 620–663.

Kurzweil, Raymond. 2000. "Ray Kurzweil's Cybernetic Poet: How it Works." *Kurzweil CyberArt Technologies*. www.kurzweilcyberart.com/poetry/rkcp_how_it_works.php

Langland-Hassan, Peter. 2020. *Explaining Imagination*. Oxford: Oxford University Press. http://doi.org/10.1093/oso/9780198815068.001.0001

Larson, Erik. 2003. *The Devil in the White City*. New York: Random House.

Le Guin, Ursula. 2016. *Words Are My Matter*. Easthampton, MA: Small Beer Press.

Liao, Shen-yi, and Tamar Gendler. 2019. "Imagination." *Stanford Encyclopedia of Philosophy*. Edited by Edward N. Zalta. http://plato.stanford.edu/imagination.

Livingston, Paisley. 2018. "Explaining 'Creativity'." In *Creativity and Philosophy*, edited by Berys Gaut and Matthew Kieran, 108–123. Abingdon: Routledge.

Mitchell, Robert. 2016. "Can Animals Imagine?" In *Routledge Handbook of Philosophy of Imagination*, edited by Amy Kind, 326–338. Abingdon: Routledge.

Mulgan, Tim. 2018. "Moral Imaginativeness, Moral Creativity, and Possible Futures." In *Creativty and Philosophy*, edited by Berys Gaut and Matthew Kieran, 350–368. Abingdon: Routledge.

Nagel, Thomas. 1974. "What is it Like to be a Bat." *Philosophical Review* 83 (4): 435–450.

Nanay, Bence. 2014. "An Experiential Account of Creativity." In *The Philosophy of Creativity: New Essays*, edited by Elliot Samuel Paul and Scott Barry Kaufman, 17–35. Oxford: Oxford University Press.

Nanay, Bence. 2016. "Imagination and Perception." In *The Routledge Handbook of Philosophy of Imagination*, edited by Amy Kind, 124–134. Abingdon: Routledge.

Nichols, Shaun. 2004. "Imagining and Believing: The Promise of a Single Code." *The Journal of Aesthetics and Art Criticism* 62 (2): 129–139.

Novitz, David. 1999. "Creativity and Constraint." *Australasian Journal of Philosophy* 77 (1): 67–82.

Nussbaum, Martha. 1997. *Cultivating Humanity*. Cambridge, MA: Harvard University Press.

Obvious. 2020. "Artificial Intelligence for Art." http://obvious-art.com/wp-content/uploads/2020/04/MANIFESTO-V2.pdf

Parfit, Derek. 1984. *Reasons and Persons*. Oxford: Oxford University Press.

Paul, Elliot Samuel, and Dustin Stokes. 2018. "Attributing Creativity." In *Creativity and Philosophy*, edited by Berys Gaut and Matthew Kieran, 193–209. Abingdon: Routledge.

Perky, Cheves West. 1910. "An Experimental Study of Imagination." *American Journal of Psychology* 21: 422–452.

Plato. 1961. "Ion." In *Plato: Collected Dialogues*, edited by Edith Hamilton and Huntington Cairns, 215–228. Princeton, NJ: Princeton University Press.

Rogers, Carl R. 1954. "Towards a Theory of Creativity." *ETC: A Review of General Semantics* 11 (4): 249–260.

Runco, Mark A., and Garrett J. Jaeger. 2012. "The Standard Definition of Creativity." *Creativity Research Journal* 24 (1): 92–96.

Ryle, Gilbert. 1949. *The Concept of Mind*. Chicago, IL: University of Chicago Press.

Scholl, Zackary. 2015. "My Poetry Generator Passed the Turing Test." https://rpiai.com/other/poetry/

Shah, Nishi, and J. David Velleman. 2005. "Doxastic Deliberation." *Philosophical Review* 114 (4): 497–534.

Simonton, Dean Keith. 2019. "Creative Genius." In *The Cambridge Handbook of Creativity*, edited by James C. Kaufman and Robert J. Sternberg, 655–676. Cambridge: Cambridge University Press.

Sinhababu, Neil. 2016. "Imagination and Belief." In *Routledge Handbook of Philosophy of Imagination*, edited by Amy Kind, 111–123. Abingdon: Routledge.

Solly, Meilan. 2018. "Christie's is First to Sell Art Made by Artificial Intelligence, But What Does That Mean?" *Smithsonian Magazine*, October 26. www.smithsonianmag.com/smart-news/christies-first-sell-art-made-artificial-intelligence-what-does-mean-180970642/

Spaulding, Shannon. 2015. "Imagination, Desire, and Rationality." *Journal of Philosophy* 112 (9): 457–476.

Stein,Morris. 1953. "Creativity and Culture." *Journal of Psychology* 36: 311–322.

Stokes, Dustin. 2019. "Mental Imagery and Fiction." *Canadian Journal of Philosophy* 49 (6): 731–754.

Stokes, Dustin. 2011. "Minimally Creative Thought." *Metaphilosophy* 42 (5): 658–681. http://doi.org/10.1111/j.1467-9973.2011.01716.x

Stokes, Dustin. 2014. "The Role of Imagination in Creativity." In *The Philosophy of Creativity: New Essays*, edited by Elliot Samuel Paul and Scott Barry Kaufman, 157–184. Oxford: Oxford University Press.

Stuart, Michael. 2019. "Everyday Scientific Imagination: A Qualitative Study of the Uses, Norms, and Pedagogy of Imagination in Science." *Science & Education* 28 (6): 711–730. http://doi.org/10.1007/s11191-019-00067-9

Stuart, Michael. 2017. "Imagination: A Sine Qua Non of Science." *Croatian Journal of Philosophy* 17 (49): 9–32.

Stuart, Michael. 2020. "The Productive Anarchy of Scientific Imagination." *Philosophy of Science* 87: 968–978.

Taliaferro, Charles, and Meredith Varie. 2018. "The Active and Passive Life of Creativity." In *Creativity and Philosophy*, edited by Berys Gaut and Matthew Kieran, 140–151. Abingdon: Routledge.

Taylor, Marjorie. 2013. "Transcending Time, Place and/or Circumstance: An Introduction." In *The Oxford Handbook of the Development of Imagination*, edited by Marjorie Taylor, 3–10. Oxford: Oxford University Press.

Taylor, Paul. 1981. "Imagination and Information." *Philosophy and Phenomenological Research* 42 (2): 205–223.

Thomson, Judith Jarvis. 1971. "A Defense of Abortion." *Philosophy and Public Affairs* 1: 47–66.

Turing, Alan. 1950. "Computing Machinery and Intelligence." *Mind* 59: 433–460.

Van Leeuwen, Neil. 2013. "The Meanings of 'Imagine' Part I: Constructive Imagination." *Philosophy Compass* 8 (3): 220–230.

Vygotsky, Lev Semenovich. 1967/2004. "Imagination and Creativity in Childhood." *Journal of Russian and East European Psychology* 42 (1): 7–97.

Walton, Kendall. 1990. *Mimesis as Make-Believe*. Cambridge, MA: Harvard University Press.

Walton, Kendall. 1994. "Morals in Fiction and Fictional Morality (1)." *Proceedings of the Aristotelian Society* 68: 27–50.

Weinberg, Jonathan, and Aaron Meskin. 2006. "Puzzling Over the Imagination: Philosophical Problems, Architectural Solutions." In *The Architecture of the Imagination*, edited by Shaun Nichols, 175–202. Oxford: Oxford University Press.

Wenzel, Christian Helmut. 2018. "The Art of Doing Mathematics." In *Creativity and Philosophy*, edited by Berys Gaut and Matthew Kieran, 313–330. Abingdon: Routledge.

White, Alan. 1990. *The Language of Imagination*. Oxford: Basil Blackwell.

Williams, Bernard. 1973. "Deciding to Believe." In *Problems of the Self*, edited by Bernard Williams, 136–151. Cambridge: Cambridge University Press.

Zeman, Adam, Michaela Dewar, and Sergio Della Sala. 2015. "Lives without Imagery – Congenital Aphantasia." *Cortex* 73: 378–380.

Acknowledgments

One of the continued joys of working at Claremont McKenna is that I get the opportunity to work with amazingly talented undergraduates. They are always an inspiration to me. I explored some of the ideas in this Element in my 2019 Advanced Seminar on Imagination; thanks to the students there for helpful discussion. I am also extremely grateful for the help of two undergraduate RAs: Julia Garbee, who assisted with background research relating to this Element, and Luis Verdin, who read through the completed manuscript and offered helpful feedback. In filming my video abstract, I also benefited greatly from the assistance of Zhutao (Flora) Li.

I also owe thanks to the two anonymous referees who provided generous feedback on an earlier draft. The final Element is significantly better as a result of their comments and suggestions. Tremendous thanks also to Keith Frankish for inviting me to write this Element, for his help throughout the process, and for his constructive feedback on my earlier draft.

Finally, I'm grateful as always to Frank Menetrez for his support throughout this process. If there are such things as creative muses, he most definitely is mine.

Cambridge Elements ≡

Philosophy of Mind

Keith Frankish

The University of Sheffield

Keith Frankish is a philosopher specializing in philosophy of mind, philosophy of psychology, and philosophy of cognitive science. He is the author of *Mind and Supermind* (Cambridge University Press, 2004) and *Consciousness* (2005), and has also edited or coedited several collections of essays, including *The Cambridge Handbook of Cognitive Science* (Cambridge University Press, 2012), *The Cambridge Handbook of Artificial Intelligence* (Cambridge University Press, 2014) (both with William Ramsey), and *Illusionism as a Theory of Consciousness* (2017).

About the Series

This series provides concise, authoritative introductions to contemporary work in philosophy of mind, written by leading researchers and including both established and emerging topics. It provides an entry point to the primary literature and will be the standard resource for researchers, students, and anyone wanting a firm grounding in this fascinating field.

Cambridge Elements $\equiv$

Philosophy of Mind

Printed in the United States
by Baker & Taylor Publisher Services